FOR THE LOVE OF
COCKTAILS

FOR THE LOVE OF
COCKTAILS

THE
EVERYDAY
GUIDE TO
**DELIGHTFUL
DRINKS**
FOR ANYONE,
ANYTIME

EVELYN CHICK

PHOTOGRAPHY BY JESSICA BLAINE SMITH

FOREWORD BY LAUREN MOTE

Figure.1

Vancouver / Toronto / Berkeley

23 24 25 26 27   5 4 3 2 1

Cataloguing data is available from Library and Archives Canada
ISBN 978-1-77327-197-2 (hbk.)

Design by Teresa Bubela
Photography by Jessica Blaine Smith

Editing by Steve Cameron
Copy editing by Pam Robertson
Proofreading by Breanne MacDonald
Indexing by Iva Cheung

Printed and bound in China by C&C Offset Printing Co.
Distributed internationally by Publishers Group West

Figure 1 Publishing Inc.
Vancouver BC Canada
www.figure1publishing.com

Figure 1 Publishing works in the traditional, unceded territory of the xʷməθkʷəy̓əm (Musqueam), Sḵwx̱wú7mesh (Squamish), and səlilwətaɬ (Tsleil-Waututh) peoples.

This book is for all the cocktail lovers, spirit or spirit-less adventurers, ultimate party hosts, and flavor enthusiasts out there. To my friends and supporters who have always inspired my creativity and pushed for me to pursue my passions through the good, the bad, and the ugly, I dedicate the celebratory sips found in these pages to you.

CONTENTS

FOREWORD

Evelyn slid a coaster on the bar and poured me a martini. She said, "This is my 'Endless English Summers' cocktail." I took a sip and, in that moment, was transported to a different time—as only taste memories can do. Evelyn looked at me, smiled, and asked, "So, where did it take you?"

My memory was of a story my mother used to tell me about her and my grandmother eating butter and rose petal sandwiches in her family garden in the English countryside. This martini was the Beefeater Gin cocktail that won Evelyn the MIXLDN title. And, it should be noted, Evelyn is masterful at creating experiences, not just drinks. But let's go back.

I've known Evelyn for years. I remember seeing her for the first time at a bar on Granville Street in Vancouver, and she was electric. She had the gift of gab with guests, and you could tell she was having the time of her life as she poured pints and simple highballs. But let's go back further.

Evelyn is a product of contrasting worlds. She moved from her homeland, Hong Kong, to Vancouver, to Toronto, imbuing her cultural story with unique flavors and experiences collected from her various homes—something that rings true for many Canadians. For those of us sitting at her bar night after night so many years later, we were regaled with Evelyn's take on building experiences through flavor.

My journey with Evelyn has been a very special one. When launching the Bittered Sling Bistro pop-up restaurant (food and drink pairing tournament), Evelyn was right there in the beginning with a few other bartending newbies-turned-luminaries. She was a competitor and a member of our internal team. My husband, chef Jonathan, and I recall late nights (and early mornings) at our dining room table sticking labels to the early editions of Bittered Sling bitters together. Evelyn's been part of our chosen family; part of our most important circle of women. She's a strong femme, sharing her stories, traditions, and curiosities with us all. Page by page in this book, you'll taste, touch, see, and experience Evelyn's journey. I have loved reading this book because I read each sentence, passage, and recipe the way Evelyn would—with fun, and flair. Her joyful attitude and simple approach make creating great drinks at home less daunting.

Being asked to write the foreword for Evelyn's book is an honor, and I'm proud to see how far she's come. She's fostering a community of home bartenders, but beyond that, this book represents the endless possibilities for professional bartenders everywhere wishing to make a lasting impact by embracing their unique histories, recording those stories through recipes, and sharing them with consumers. Bartenders possess the power to create memorable experiences, and whether at the bar or through books like this, we also have the ability to teach and to help home bartenders commemorate daily celebrations. I'll cheers to that.

LAUREN MOTE

Co-Founder, Bittered Sling
Director of On-Trade, PATRÓN Tequila

INTRODUCTION

My hospitality journey began at a very young age. My grandparents ran a seafood restaurant in Kowloon, Hong Kong, and I recall having an absolute riot in the kitchen. I'd be at my grandmother's elbow while she cooked, sneaking tastes, and watching intently as she plated her beautiful meals. I was fascinated by the rolling, stretching, chopping, and searing going on in the kitchen, and I was equally enamored with ritualistic activities like Chinese tea service—which lasted for hours at my home. My nanny was Filipino, and she cooked with a multitude of flavors—acid, sweet, heat, spice, umami—that have stuck with me to this day. When I was eight years old, I insisted on pouring my dad's whiskies and chilling the wine for my mother, and while the adults argued about stocks and real estate over baijiu on the main table, I was always awkwardly setting up my own "parties" on the side.

I immigrated to Canada when I was thirteen. Going from a big city full of culture, color, and flavor to a smaller, more relaxed environment was an adjustment but I quickly acclimatized. It was during my time as a starving artist in university that I got my first taste of the modern service industry. I relish those early years being a late-night dweller, thriving in the fast-cash and free-spirited club lifestyle. It was around this time that I won a draw for a trip to go to the Kentucky Bourbon Trail. Taking that journey and learning about the history and the craft that goes into the making of the spirit sparked a fire in me. I started taking bartending a bit more seriously, but not so seriously that I didn't experiment with flavors and techniques.

I loved being unconventional. I'd mix and match flavors—inspired deep down by my culinary mentors—and I'd use anything as a bar tool. Mason jars, cone pasta strainers, and chopsticks were all just as good in a pinch as standard-issue barware if it meant getting the spirit from the bottle, through my creative process, and into the glass. Improvisation became a key theme of mine.

From those nascent days of creating off-the-cuff cocktails, I became a student of all things bar and beverage. I now hold top-level certifications in wine, spirits, and beer, not to mention many other categories to do with mixing. I've competed in mixing competitions nationally and globally, and in 2015 I was named best in the world against entrants from thirty-five other countries in making a brand-specific cocktail for Beefeater Gin.

I was on a career high. I was part of the team that opened one of the most experimental cocktail bars in Canada, I was beverage director of a large hospitality group, I consulted for brands and anyone who desired a good cocktail program. I wrote recipes for publications and traveled often, working with farm-to-table chefs and sharing herbs, produce, and materials for the bar. It was simply amazing.

Then the global pandemic hit.

Like many of you reading, the pandemic completely rocked me to the core. I felt no direction and I lost the desire to create. My love of hosting had nowhere to go. If people could no longer enjoy the cocktails that moved through my fingers and were served to them by me, in a physical space, what and who was my vocation for?

The pandemic forced me to slow down and reflect on the reason I'd gotten into this crazy business in the first place: putting flavors together and making easy-to-find pantry items work in new and unexpected ways. You know that winning cocktail I was talking about? It had one key ingredient that mimicked the taste and smell of fresh cut grass after a nice morning rain, and that one ingredient alone contained *nine* different ingredients—excuse me?

Such beautiful and inspirational moments in my life, the ones I continually come back to, all have one commonality—they were about the simple joy of sharing flavors in approachable ways. And that is my goal with *For the Love of Cocktails*. I want you to experience a world of flavors and sensations simply and easily. Unexpected delights are at your fingertips. It's not about the complexity of the construction of the cocktail, the rarity of the spirits, or the quality of the barware you have. It is about joyful pursuit, being unafraid to make mistakes, and the willingness to try something new. And of course, if and when you can, sharing these moments with those closest to you.

Thank you for trusting in me to guide you on your next after-work cocktail, celebration drinks, canna-curious adventure, or backyard get-together. I hope this book will help you experience something different, perhaps enlighten your senses or discover something unique. I wish you confidence and joy as you become a better drink maker, and I hope that you feel curiosity, surprise, and happiness as you move to create your own take on my recipes—embarking on your drink curating journey. I have always believed that one sip or one bite can change one's momentary existence. I hope that you can create some of these beautiful moments for yourself by using this book.

THE NITTY GRITTY

I'm all for experimentation, but before we dive into making tinctures, garnishes, and refreshing cocktails, we first need to cover some basics. The creation of a drink is similar to the creation of a dish: without understanding the "why" behind the tools and techniques you use, the vessel you're serving it in, and the base spirits you select, you won't be able to fully unlock the potential of what is possible. And it is right at your fingertips—so let's set you up for success!

TOOLS OF THE TRADE

There's a misconception that a home bar needs to be stocked with high-end bar tools only found at cocktail specialty stores for you to make a sound variety of cocktails. I'm just going to go ahead and correct that thought. Yes, having access to all the gear in the world is fabulous—but any good bartender will be able to whip up a balanced and delicious drink with some creativity, intent, and purpose, no matter the tools available. After all, once you know what *can* be achieved with the best gear, you can begin to replicate it with whatever you have on hand.

Cocktail Shaker

Simply, for drinks that need to be shaken—which is done to simultaneously chill the drink and dilute the spirits with water from the ice.

Boston Shaker: I prefer using a two-piece "tin on tin" Boston shaker—stainless steel, low chance of breakage, and keeps your drink cold. Boston shakers require a strainer and are great for making multiple drinks.

Cobbler Shaker: This three-piece shaker tends to be smaller and contains a built-in strainer under the cap. These are popular in Japanese bartending for a three-point shake. They yield better aeration and texture in a small-volume drink by chilling the cocktail quicker and with less dilution.

IN A PINCH

Consider using a gym bottle or a mason jar. Hell, I've even used a Tupperware container before. Essentially, you can use anything for shaking and pouring your cocktail so long as it has enough space for ice to freely flow around and has a lid that will hold the ice back while you strain.

Cocktail Mixing Glass and Bar Spoon

A cocktail mixing glass is for drinks that need delicate handling and a more finessed chilling, like a Martini or a Manhattan. The mixing glass is glass or metal with a pour spout (kind of like a science beaker), and drinks are quickly chilled in it with the help of a bar spoon to guide the liquid and ice around the glass. The bar spoon's twisty handle makes it easy to pinch between your fingers and helps swirl the drink. When guiding the liquid and ice around the mixing glass, the idea is to brace the back of the bar spoon against the inside of the glass to prevent you from agitating the liquid too much. Remember, this is a finessed chilling. A mixing glass should fit at least one 3-ounce cocktail plus ice.

IN A PINCH

A 16-ounce beer glass and a chopstick are suitable stand-ins. The chopstick does the job, but it is only a stir stick and not as versatile as the bar spoon, as the bar spoon's design helps with the movement of ice in the glass and the spoon can also be used to measure small amounts of ingredients.

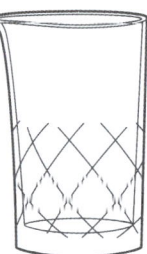

③ Measuring Jigger

A measuring jigger is the bartender's measuring cup—but with smaller, more accurate measurements. Pictured here is a Japanese jigger, which is easy to fit in between your fingers so the fluid from it can easily slide into your receiving vessel.

IN A PINCH

A baker's measuring spoon will do. In Canada and the US, we usually measure in imperial fluid ounces, whereas measuring spoons usually provide both cook's measurements and metric measurements in milliliters. But so long as you are following the measuring guide on page 47, you are good to go!

④ Hawthorne Strainer

A Hawthorne strainer is a flat metal disk with a built-in coil spring. It is used with a Boston shaker to hold back ice, fruit, or herbs so there aren't any floating pieces to get stuck in your (or your guest's) teeth. It also allows you to keep "old ice" from going from the shaker to the glass, preventing overdilution.

IN A PINCH

A large, slotted spoon nestled against the edge of your shaking vessel will filter out debris and ice just fine. Not as elegant, but it does the trick.

 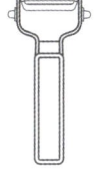

⑤ Potato Peeler

Yes, the humble potato peeler can be the tool that helps make or break a cocktail. You can use it to create a simple citrus garnish. Not only does the garnish add aromatics where needed, for instance to highlight delicate notes in a cocktail when adding pure juice would overwhelm other flavors and throw the whole cocktail out of balance, it also acts as a fantastic way to guide the recipient's senses. To learn to create a citrus garnish, head to page 48.

IN A PINCH

No peeler in the house? Then a sharp paring knife and a cutting board will work. Hold your citrus perpendicular to the board and run your knife down the side, taking only the peel off. If a lot of pith is left on it (the white part that contains a lot of bitterness), simply shave it down by laying the peel flat on the cutting board and sliding the knife away from the direction of your hand.

6

Elbow Juicer

Making juice with an elbow juicer (or a hand press)—which is exactly what it sounds like, putting some elbow grease into the extraction—is superior to store-bought juice. Pressed juice adds texture and aromatics to your cocktail, especially with citrus, as the sweet oils from the rind will add another dimension to your drink. I recommend you cut the fruit lengthwise, so it can naturally fold into the cavity of the juicer. Then place it with the flesh facing the perforated bottom, and squeeze firmly.

> **— IN A PINCH —**
>
> If you don't have a juicer, simply cut your citrus in quarters rather than halves, and squeeze the fruit over a fork to strain out the seeds.

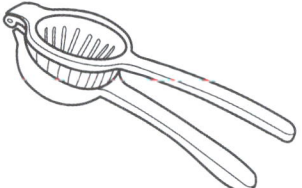

7

Cone Strainer

If you are making infusions (and I hope you do!), the process typically requires the solids from your infusion to be strained out. A fine cone strainer not only holds back the unwanted solids (like a tea strainer for tea leaves), but makes bottling easy with its directional gravitational pull.

> **— IN A PINCH —**
>
> A cheesecloth helps strain out finer solids like zested lime so there is no grittiness or other unwanted texture in the infused or cooked liquids that will get into your cocktail.

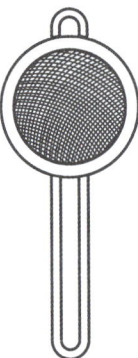

Ice Mold

Considering the shape, size, and density of your ice will help take your drinks to the next level, so investing in a good ice mold is something that a cocktail enthusiast should consider. A large 2-inch x 2-inch mold is great for those drinks you pour over a large cube of ice (a king cube!) in the glass. A 1-inch x 1-inch mold is terrific for stirred drinks, as well as those that you build in the glass—like an Old Fashioned—which benefit from slower dilution time. I typically use silicone ice molds as they are malleable and easy to clean.

IN A PINCH

Why a good ol' plastic ice cube tray will certainly work. Make sure you fill the water right to the brim. The most important thing with ice is that you use the amounts called for in the recipe method.

SOME NICE TO HAVES

Even the experienced home bartender can improve their home setup. None of these things are mandatory, but they are certainly extra helpful if you have them.

 ### High-Powered Blender

When it comes to using fresh fruits and herbs, there is nothing easier than to use the "cold extract" method so the colors and flavors of the produce remain fresh, especially when it comes to making syrups. I personally prefer a blender that has a range of options for chopping and blending, plus time guides, like the Ninja Foodi Power Blender. Find syrup recipes in the Sweeteners chapter (see page 183).

Lewis Bag

Who is Lewis? I don't know who the namesake of this tool is, but the Lewis Bag is a canvas pouch that, way back when, was used by banks to transport coins. Before perfectly shaped ice from freezers was a thing, bartenders had to smash natural ice blocks with a mallet to get pieces suitable for drink-making. The canvas bag was prized for its durability and its ability to absorb water. Today it is an easy way to achieve crushed ice at home. Smashing ice is also a great party trick and conveniently doubles as a host stress-relief aid. Best part? Great for tiki-style drinks that contain higher-proof spirits or textures that require an added amount of dilution.

Sous Vide or Immersion Circulator

For those curious cats who love a good infusion (an injection of flavor into sugars or liquids through the addition of an extractable base ingredient, like fruits and herbs), this device is great to chop down the time infusion takes as well as create deeper, more integrated flavors. You will also require an airtight, non-reactive container like a mason jar or vacuum-sealed bag.

GLASSWARE

As a child, I was always fascinated with beautiful plates and glassware. And as an adult, I'm no different, because a properly curated serving vessel very much dictates the level of enjoyment a person can have with a cocktail. Sometimes your glassware can act as an extravagant garnish, but most of the time the glass you pick should be based purely on the volume and style of the drink. Since this book is all about making drinks for appreciative moments, I'm going to give you some guidelines in the following pages as to what glassware to get for each drink, occasion, and situation.

To make the recipes in this book, you will only need variations of four styles of glassware. I've listed them below.

①  **Rocks Glass**

Typically used for an Old Fashioned, Negroni, or Margarita, and it can hold 9–12 ounces. Ideally, your rocks glass should fit rocks—ice—and a good one can hold at least four cubes of ice (1 inch x 1 inch) along with liquid. This allows you to build the cocktail in the glass, if you wish. Most often, this glass is used for cocktails without lengtheners (extra, non-alcoholic ingredients—soda, for instance—that create a larger-volume drink) and delivers a more intense, shorter cocktail that needs ice for dilution. They are easy to find and can pretty much hold anything stirred or shaken on the rocks. It is the workhorse of cocktail glasses.

② **Collins Glass**

Tall and slender, this is a great vessel of choice for Mojitos, a Tom Collins, or a Swizzle. This style of glass is perfect for drinks that need a bit of lengthener, and its slender shape holds the carbonation in fizzes longer. Classic Collins glasses usually hold 10–14 ounces. Similar to a Collins glass is the highball glass. It is also tall and slender, but holds less volume, usually 7–9 ounces.

③ **Coupe Glass**

This is the quintessential glass for cocktails served up (a cocktail that is shaken or stirred with ice but served without it). Originally used for Champagne (which changed in the 1970s for some reason), it has a saucer-like form and curves up on the side to form a shallow bowl. Coupe glasses can typically hold 5–8 ounces and are used for cocktails served up so that the flavors of the drink intensify with each successive sip. The stem allows you to hold onto the glass without warming up the cocktail by handling the bowl.

④ **Wine Glass**

I can go on and on and on about how certain wine varietals should be put in certain shapes of wine glasses. But hey, this is a cocktail book! I love using wine glasses for Spanish-style Gin and Tonics or spritz-style drinks. The large volume of a wine glass (you should aim to use glasses ranging 12–18 ounces) is nice to use for building the cocktail in the glass, as its size allows you to swirl the drink in the glass to open up the concentrated liquids. Also, because a wine glass typically has a narrower mouth than body, it will direct the aromatics of your cocktail upwards toward the drinker for an optimal whiff. Damn! Who's craving a spritz now?

HOSTING A PARTY

There is something nostalgic and interactive about serving up a big ol' bowl of fun when your friends roll up. I mean, there is a whole chapter on it later in the book, but here for you now are two glassware must haves.

5 Elegant Pitchers

The purpose of a pitcher is to hold a large volume of liquid you want to pour into cups, and the spout is to let the liquid out while holding back any ice or debris. I use a pitcher for those large serves that I plan on pouring over ice, always accompanied by a large wooden spoon to agitate it, much the same way the ladle works in the punch bowl. I usually find these at vintage stores—and the best come accompanied with matching glasses that hold a smaller volume, perfect for sipping and sharing. But honestly, a plastic beer pitcher will also work just fine!

6 Punch Bowls

Not unlike in my youthfully exuberant days, when me and my friends threw all sorts of juices into a "king's cup" and called it a day, a good punch bowl should be big. A great starting point for a four-person serving is a glass bowl that holds at least 3 liters of liquid with ice, and has enough room to throw some delightful garnishes on top. Make sure your bowl is neither too shallow nor too deep. You want the accompanying ladle to be able to scoop up a good mix of liquid, ice, and herbs and fruit, and for it to sit in the bowl with the handle free so that it is easy to agitate throughout the party.

Any successful home bar should contain a selection of spirits and alcohols that you like to drink. It doesn't have to be complicated or overstocked, but it must be purposeful, good quality, and—the most obvious—booze you like! Picking a spirit is such a personal experience. People who love herbal flavor profiles will probably gravitate toward white spirit categories like gin, tequila, or blanco rums. Those who like warm vanilla notes will probably appreciate an aged spirit like whiskey or a brandy. Either way, pick your battles and don't feel like you must carry everything. Most importantly, treat yourself by investing in smaller amounts of good products. You'll thank me for that tip over and over and over again.

VODKA

Typically, vodka is a neutral grain spirit distilled to be high proof and then watered down to bottling strength (minimum 40 percent alcohol by volume—or ABV—in North America). While most vodkas are made from grain, it can also be made with other ingredients like potatoes and fruit, which can provide for some unique flavors beyond the citrus and black pepper notes commonly associated with the spirit. No matter what the notes in the vodka, its main appeal for many people is its relatively neutral taste, so it is an easy sell for a mixer as it takes on pretty much any flavor added to it. If you are new to cocktails, this may just be the spirit category for you to start with.

MY FAVES

DILLON'S SMALL BATCH VODKA is triple distilled and made with 100 percent Canadian rye. It has great viscosity, and subtle savory notes, making this the perfect spirit for a dry vodka Gibson (a Martini garnished with a pickled onion).

HAKU VODKA is made with hakumai—100 percent white rice from Japan. It is double distilled and filtered through bamboo charcoal. The resulting liquid carries a citrus and floral aroma, and is great in stirred, spirit-forward cocktails.

ABSOLUT VODKA is produced in Sweden and is an everyday workhorse. Made with winter wheat, it is a full-bodied spirit with just a hint of dried fruit at the end. Absolut Vodka's flavored expressions are also fantastic and are an easy way to serve up some fun cocktails at home.

Apple 'n' Herbs, p. 60

GIN

Known for its botanical expression—each specific to the distiller who makes it—all gins have the steady profile of the evergreen note from distilled juniper berries, which is mandatory for the spirit to be classified as gin. There are many styles of gin, from a classic London Dry Gin (which has pronounced juniper notes combined with classic botanicals like citrus peel, coriander, and angelica root), Old Tom (which brings a slight hint of sweetness), Genever (which imparts a little extra texture from its grain base of barley, corn, or rye—or a combination of them), Plymouth (which has an intense aromatic nature and bold taste) to New Western Dry Gins (which are innovative in their botanical makeups). As you can see, each category offers a different characteristic for your cocktails and the base gin you choose to use can make the same cocktail—from something as complex as a Fog Cutter to something as simple as a classic Martini—taste dramatically different. As a massive gin lover, this is where I stock up.

MY FAVES

HENDRICK'S GIN is flavored with cucumber and rose essence, making a unique gin. It also has notes of elderflower, lemon, and orange, and is copper and column stilled. For those who are just starting to enjoy this spirit, Hendrick's is a great jumping off point as it is light in juniper notes.

SPIRIT OF YORK GIN is loaded with fifteen select botanicals, and has a good base of juniper, cinnamon, coriander, and fennel seed

It is crisp, refreshing, and great for a classic Gin and Tonic or a stirred Gimlet-style drink. Spirit of York also produces a hawthorn berry gin with delicious berry notes infused with maple syrup.

AVIATION GIN is an American Dry Gin (a New Western) with less pronounced juniper notes than some, and with added botanicals of lavender, anise seed, and sarsaparilla. Steeped and distilled through a copper pot still, this gin

boasts some floral qualities and a nice texture that is good for tall classics like the Tom Collins.

PLYMOUTH NAVY STRENGTH GIN sits at 57 percent ABV, and as a result is one of my favorite Martini gins. With only seven botanicals, this gin plays well with other ingredients yet offers an intensely bold and aromatic flavor profile.

Group G&T, p. 166

Big Pony Swizzle, p. 69

RUM

Growing in popularity, rum is distilled from sugarcane products (mainly molasses) and varies with influences of terroir. The spectrum of rum expressions is wide, from grassy and delicately citrusy white rums to aged dark rums with beautiful flavors of molasses, baking spices, and grasses that sing to the tiki gods but also lend well to a stirred cocktail. Then there are spiced rums, which offer some added depth to the already complex spirit, and which are ever so popular in cocktails and punches—and even work well in a simple highball.

MY FAVES

WORTHY PARK SINGLE ESTATE RESERVE is a delicious Jamaican amber rum that comes in just above 90 proof at 45 percent ABV. Full of ripe banana, mango, and slightly sweet ginger notes, I love using this in a long tropical drink as it holds its own when paired with other juicy ingredients.

DIPLOMATICO RESERVA EXCLUSIVA RUM is a column and pot stilled rum with notes of chocolate, coffee, and deep brown maple. This versatile rum is great for shaken cocktails that contain tropical fruit and for stirred cocktails, like a classic El Presidente, in which it complements the earthiness and the orange peel elements.

HAVANA CLUB 3 YEAR OLD RUM is a slightly aged rum that takes on a pale, golden color and imparts the smallest hint of oak. In a Daiquiri it lends some vanilla flavors without losing the bright citrus components.

AGAVE SPIRITS

This category includes tequila and mezcal, as well as some lesser-known spirits like raicilla. The common thread among all of them is that they are expressions of the agave plant, which takes 6–8 years to grow to maturity before it can be turned into what I think is the purest spirit expression of what Mother Nature provides us. Agave spirits are not only delicately beautiful and unique, they are the fastest growing spirit category in the business.

Tequila

A lot of people, including myself, have had bad experiences with tequila. Most of those tequilas we avoid are mixto, which means they contain coloring, thickeners, and other non-agave sugars added during and after distillation. It is likely these additives that explain the massive hangovers we collectively associate with tequila. However, from the soft and citrus-forward tequilas from agaves grown in the clay-rich soils of Los Altos, to the peppery and earthy spirit that arises from the volcanic soils of El Valle, to all the expressions in between, there truly is something for everyone. The lesson is to spend a couple more dollars on high-quality stuff, and make sure to look for 100 percent blue Weber agave—you will forever be changed.

MY FAVES

PATRON SILVER TEQUILA is a triple-distilled, blended tequila fermented with agave fibers, unaged. It is my go-to for bright tequila drinks like a standard Paloma, as it highlights the herbaceous quality of the agave but does not sacrifice its tropical, citrus, and floral notes.

HERRADURA REPOSADO TEQUILA is a reposado (which means rested), and this particular expression pioneered the technique and the category. It is aged in ex-bourbon barrels for eleven months, and the wood imparts a hint of vanilla and sweet spice that is paired with flavors of green pepper and warm baking spices. It is absolutely stunning. I love to showcase all those delicious notes in a Tommy's Margarita, made of three ingredients: Herradura Reposado, lime juice, and agave syrup.

Pineapple Blanco, p. 118

Mezcal

The origin of mezcal dates to the sixteenth century. Unlike tequila, which should only be made with blue Weber agave, this spirit can be distilled from over 150 species of agave plants, the majority of them coming from the state of Oaxaca—and the most popular being the espadin varietal. The pina (or heart) of this plant is buried in pit ovens, giving the spirit its distinctively smoky aroma. Like tequila, the taste and smell of mezcal varies between microclimates where the agave was grown, making each expression unique. The distinct aroma of mezcal can be jarring, but once you get past the initial intensity, the flavors that lie within—from floral to green pepper and smoke—are incredible.

MY FAVES

SOMBRA MEZCAL is a fantastic introduction to mezcal. It is distilled in the Sierra Madre mountains, in the highlands of San Juan del Rio, using the wild, organic agave varietal espadin. Distilled in copper pot stills, this spirit imparts notes of earthy minerality paired with evergreen notes of pine.

That profile is exactly why I picked it for one of my favorite cocktails in this book, S'up Wit Dat? (see page 81).

DEL MAGUEY TOBALA MEZCAL is made from the tobala species of agave, which is the smallest of the species and eight times smaller than the average espadin (meaning it takes the pina from eight tobalas to create this spirit versus one pina for espadin-based mezcals). Del Maguey Tobala is truly a labor of love. The use of this small varietal produces a fruit-forward spirit with floral, tropical notes. It is incredible on its own or in a stirred cocktail.

WHISK(E)Y

An undeniably vast category carrying flavors from butterscotch to peeled citrus to stewed fruit and coffee, to name a few. Depending on the expression, there really is an endless number of possibilities to using this malted distillate in your cocktails. I've only focused on whiskey from the US, Canada, and Scotland, but there are plenty of fabulous whiskey expressions from around the world, including smooth, triple-distilled Irish whiskey to elegant and subtle Japanese whiskey to fruit-forward and lightly smoked Indian whisky, and so many more! Find the expression you like, and don't be afraid to branch out. It's a big world!

Nutty Doctor, p. 75

American

American whiskey, especially bourbon, is consistently in the forefront of the cocktail world, being the base for classics like the Old Fashioned and the Manhattan. There isn't a cocktail aficionado who does not have at least one bourbon preference, and the reason why it is so popular is largely due to the strict rules that depict quality and rarity, depending on the spirit purveyor. According to the Distilled Spirits Council of the United States, bourbon must be made with at least 51 percent corn, and aged in charred, new American oak barrels for at least two years. The mash bill, or the distribution of grain proportions, and the level of char in the barrel are what influence the flavor of the spirit. American rye, on the other hand, needs to be at least 51 percent rye, with other ingredients in the mash consisting of corn and malted barley. This style of rye offers a bold and slightly peppery, spicy note, which makes for a fantastic classic Manhattan as it complements the rooty, bittersweet undertones of your choice of vermouth.

MY FAVES

ANGEL'S ENVY is a Kentucky straight bourbon whiskey finished in Port casks. This powerhouse bourbon is loaded with flavor due to its unique cask finish, featuring luscious maple and vanilla notes and some toasty nuttiness on top of the Port influence.

Angel's Envy is a beautiful choice for fresh, shaken Bucks (typically containing ginger beer or ale) or floral, stirred cocktails.

WOODFORD RESERVE BOURBON consists mostly of corn, followed by rye, and finally malted barley, which creates a profile of mellow notes of cinnamon spice and chocolate. It is very easy to integrate this Kentucky staple into cocktails and it is a fantastic choice for a classic Old Fashioned.

Guerrilla Girls, p. 123

Canadian

Canadian whisky is an extremely underrated category. It is incredibly versatile, offering a wide range of flavors and textures, from smooth and mellow corn-heavy blends to bold and full-bodied rye-dominant ones. Part of the reason Canadian whisky is underrated is perception. While generally these spirits are, by law, made with cereal grains—corn and rye being the front-runners of choice—Canadian whiskies are allowed up to 9.09 percent additives in their malt bill, which allows a misconception of the quality of product. Canadian whisky must be aged a minimum of three years in charred barrels. This category features robust notes of pepper and baking spice, as well as the sometimes-bright hint of citrus and the softness of caramel. Canadian whisky is truly a dynamic spirit.

MY FAVES

LOT NO. 40 100% POT STILL RYE WHISKY is my go-to 100 percent rye grain whisky. It boasts an amber color with notes of maple and vanilla, plus toasty cinnamon and other baking spices, and a hint of nuttiness. I have included a couple of cocktails in this book that use this delicious elixir, which is equally good for shaken or stirred cocktails.

PIKE CREEK 10 YEAR OLD WHISKY is a Canadian corn whisky blend finished in rum barrels, providing notes of honey, raisins, and pecans. This whisky is great on the rocks as an after-dinner sipper or mixed in a tropical drink that normally uses rum for an unexpected, but welcome, kick.

Scotch

Scotch whiskies, ranging from blended to single malt, will provide cocktails with an array of flavors like butterscotch, peat smoke, earth, and wood finishes that are unachievable in other categories. Scotch single malts can only be distilled from malts originating from one single distillery. They are distinctive and grouped by regions in the country, and the taste is very discernable from one terroir to another. Highlands and Speyside Scotches make up the widest variations in style with rounded and dry whiskies and a slight peatiness. The Lowlands offer softer, more delicate flavors; Islay expressions are famous for their peaty, saline, and umami quality; and Campbeltown brings a distinctive seaside character to the whiskey. Blended Scotch simply means that the liquid can come from multiple distilleries, and does not take away from the quality of the product.

Traditionally, Scotch has such a stuffy, do-not-mix vibe, and that's precisely why I love to reach for it when making cocktails. Cocktails are meant to be fun—I say break the rules and let stiff perceptions fall by the wayside! I grew up watching my father mix blended Scotch with honeyed Japanese green tea in a highball glass. What a pioneer!

MY FAVES

GLENLIVET FOUNDER'S RESERVE SCOTCH is a Speyside whisky with notes of stone fruit, orange, Sherry, and toffee. It has impeccable texture and some creamy toffee notes that make it perfect for a Bobby Burns.

MONKEY SHOULDER SCOTCH is a blended malt made with Scotch from the distilleries of Balvenie, Glenfiddich, and Kininvie. Each batch is blended with nine casks from each distillery and, as such, is labeled "Batch 27." Monkey Shoulder is a rich, golden yellow color with notes of tropical fruit and vanilla, and it has a slightly floral undertone. This whisky pairs immensely well with Sherries and stone fruit.

CHIVAS REGAL 12 YEAR OLD SCOTCH is a blended Highlands malt with honey notes, smoky vanilla, black pepper, and nuttiness. This is one of my father's go-to whiskies. With a long finish and some fruity pear and apple qualities, this whisky is great for a shaken or stirred cocktail.

LAPHROAIG QUARTER CASK SCOTCH is arguably one of the hardest Scotches to get a non–Scotch drinker to be on board with, but it is also one of the most beautiful expressions of Islay whisky. Matured in small quarter casks, this whisky smells of the peatiest of peat bogs (that's a good thing) and is simultaneously pleasantly sweet, imbuing a caramelized nose with notes of bright citrus. I love adding just a quarter or half ounce of this whisky to a fruit-forward cocktail for an element of surprise.

BRANDY

Brandy, by definition, is a distillate most famously made from grape musk but it can also be made from other fruits. As a category it is vast and plentiful, with styles all over the world, and flavors ranging from clean and herbal fruit notes, like a Peruvian pisco, to chocolate, raisins, leather, and fig, like an XO (extra old) Cognac. The infamous French brandy, which is geographically protected, helped kick-start the cross-Atlantic triangle trade, taking over from the fortified wines mentioned in the next section due to ease of transport. So, brandy is not just fancy juice, but has played a significant role in aiding the development of the global process of distillation itself.

MY FAVES

D'USSÉ VSOP COGNAC is made by one of the oldest Cognac houses in the world. If you have a couple bucks to spare, this VSOP (very special old pale) is exceptional in quality. With notes of rich limousine wood, baking spices, and a lingering floral touch, it is fantastic to have as a sipper. The uniqueness of Cognac is that it must be made from white grapes in its strictly approved growing regions; it must also go through double distillation. For a VS expression, it must be aged at least two years, and for a VSOP, at least four years.

CAMPO DE ENCANTO PISCO MOSCATEL is a single-vineyard pisco made from one of the eight grape varietals used to produce pisco in Peru. This expression truly lets the Moscato grape shine, with aromas of jasmine, lily, green apple, and pear. It also boasts a touch of earthiness and honey at the end, making it perfect to pair with some citrus and texture like you will find in a good Pisco Sour.

FORTIFIED WINES

As a wine nerd and sommelier, I find this category is seriously underrated. It carries some of the most diverse flavors you can use in a cocktail, ones that other categories simply don't have. Fortified wine means that a distilled spirit has been added to a wine base to stop fermentation, hence fortifying the wine. There are three regionally specific fortified wines: Sherry, made from wines in the Jerez region of Spain; Port (or Porto), from the Douro region of Portugal; and Madeira, from the Portuguese island of the same name that sits off the coast of Morocco. The most beautiful thing about this category is that often it requires time to make, just as wines take time to age. And that adds to the overall complexity of each drop. Ever had toasted walnut, dried figs, thyme, chocolate, and coffee all in the same tasting note? Seriously, you need to get on board because I can go on forever. Fortified wines usually sit at around 17–20 percent alcohol, which means it's best kept in the fridge to prevent oxidation and to preserve freshness.

MY FAVES

TIO PEPE FINO SHERRY is made from Palomino Fino grapes from the González Byass family in Jerez. It is an incredible fortified wine to have on its own; bone dry with hints of minerality and grass, it pairs well with cured meat or oysters.

In a cocktail, pair it with white spirit–based drinks to add a hint of salinity.

LUSTAU LOS ARCOS AMONTILLADO SHERRY is another Sherry made with Palomino Fino grapes. However, it is an oxidized expression of the fortified wine that brings with it a rich, nutty flavor. I have used this as a base for low-ABV cocktails and also as a lengthener and additive to whiskey drinks, to yield a softer, rounder palate with toffee and marzipan notes.

AROMATIZED WINES

This is a subcategory of fortified wines that are infused with botanicals, roots, or spices, either in the base wine or the added spirit. Vermouth is by far the star of this category. Originating in Italy, and now made globally, vermouth is set apart from other aromatized wines by the inclusion of wormwood (or extracts from the wormwood genus, *Artemisia*). Other popular varieties of aromatized wines include Americano, Quinquina, Chinato, and Lillet, a French aromatized wine with slight flavors of bitter roots like quinine, plus orange peel and lime zest. You may have heard of it as a key ingredient in the Vesper Martini popularized by James Bond.

MY FAVES

MARTINI BIANCO VERMOUTH is filtered from Trebbiano (an Italian white wine), sweetened with beet sugars, fortified with a neutral grain spirit, and flavored with herbs. It is clean, and slightly sweet with notes of vanilla flower. Serve it alone with tonic or use it to enhance the flavors of a shaken or stirred cocktail, as it stands up to both white and dark spirits.

GUERRA ROJO VERMOUTH is a gorgeous medium-bodied fortified wine, with notes of dark cacao, dried pine, licorice, bitter orange, and dark fruits like plum and black currant. Produced from Mencia and Godello grapes, this vermouth is definitely the dark spirit whisperer, and adds depth and texture to a classic like a Rob Roy. For a low-ABV digestif, simply add some soda with orange peel aromatics and you're all set.

COCCHI AMERICANO is an aromatized white wine from the Italian region of Piedmont. It contains notes of rich chinchona bark, honeysuckle, gentian (a bittersweet root historically used for medicinal purposes), and citrus. Use it as a heavier-bodied and sweeter alternative to Lillet in any Martini.

Open Sesame, p. 111

LIQUEURS

A good home bar should have a liqueur or two, whether it be store bought or homemade. A liqueur is simply a spirit with additional flavorings such as fruits, herbs, and spices and the addition of sugar. Basic liqueurs are not difficult to make but here are some staples that have been around for decades.

Fig Dreams, p. 64

Herbal and Bitter Liqueurs

Herbal and bitter liqueurs contain some sweetness but most importantly a mixture of herbs, roots, and peels. They provide freshness, roundness, and depth to a cocktail. This category, descended from herbal medicine, dates as far back as the thirteenth century and includes bartender's favorites like Chartreuse and amaro. Often the ABV is in the 26–53 percent range and, depending on the product, the liqueur can make a perfect digestif on its own.

GREEN CHARTREUSE is an herbal liqueur and is truly a magical and natural green elixir that contains 132—132!—botanicals. Its fascinating story dates to the 1800s, and, to this day, it is still owned and made by monks of the Carthusian Order. I've had the distinct pleasure of visiting the distillery in the French Alps. It was a breathtaking experience to see the grounds and the cellars—especially the aging barrels, some of which are more than a hundred years old! Green Chartreuse is a secret weapon for balancing out classics with just the right amount of herbal quality, including notes of lime, mint, thyme, aniseed, and even ginger. Its counterpart, Yellow Chartreuse, is also fantastic when available; it has a honeyed flavor and is slightly lower in ABV.

FERNET-BRANCA is a famous Italian bitter made with thirty roots and herbs, including saffron, chamomile, and gentian. It has a black liquorice undertone with a bold, bone-dry, minty finish. This is the big bad bitter that everyone is nervous about. However, if used wisely, Fernet-Branca gives incredible structure and backbone to a drink, stirred or shaken.

CYNAR. I can't stress how much I love this sh*t! It is an Italian aperitif (and also can be considered a digestif due to its rooty, medicinal quality) and is flavored with artichoke leaves—yes, artichoke leaves. Don't let it fool you. Cynar's vegetal qualities are coupled with notes of peppermint, walnut, and cinnamon spice. The little bit of bitterness it has also helps with citrus-forward drinks. It can be served as is on the rocks, in a juniper-forward gin cocktail, or in a shaken drink. Cynar's versatility is nearly endless; you should certainly snag yourself a cheeky bottle.

The Eddy, p. 124

Aperitivo and Floral Liqueurs

These are light and bright in style, and are typically 11–24 percent alcohol. The most well-known aperitivo cocktail is an Aperitivo Spritz, which is simply aperitivo mixed with soda and quality sparkling wine, which we will dig into in another chapter. These liqueurs serve the purpose of opening up a palate before your typical meal—unlike the bitter, herbal liqueurs listed above, which tend to be heavier in body and contain darker notes.

MY FAVES

CAMPARI is undeniably famous in the cocktail world. From its vibrant red color to its being a part of some of the most well-known classics like the Negroni and the Americano, Campari is a must-have for any home bar. With a depth of flavor that includes bittersweet notes of oranges and some baking spices, and its mid-range ABV, it provides a great backbone for cocktails that need a slightly bitter kick.

ST-GERMAIN ELDERFLOWER LIQUEUR, often called the bartender's ketchup, provides an easy way to add a natural floral quality—inclusive of zesty lemon meringue, pear, and sometimes lychee—to stirred or shaken cocktails without adding too much sweetness. It is made with hand-picked elderflowers that are macerated in brandy.

NON-ALCOHOLIC DISTILLATES

I am all about providing an inclusive drinking environment to your dinner guests or at your bar, and non-alcoholic distillates are far from a trend; the surface of this category has barely been scratched. Here are some of my favorites that provide depth of flavor and some texture to your cocktails without sacrificing quality.

MY FAVES

LUMETTE! LONDON DRY is a distilled spirit with an incredible amount of botanicals. It rivals a standard gin, featuring notes of juniper, lemon, and star anise (and a healthy amount of it), all without alcohol!

LYRE'S has a multitude of offerings that truly cover all the bases. Their impressive roster includes a spiced, dealcoholized dark cane spirit that has notes of caramel, molasses, and nuts with some cacao and baking spices on the back end. Try it in a classic Mai Tai recipe and I guarantee it will blow your mind.

SEEDLIP and its stable of expressions are the original non-alcoholic spirits. My favorite is Spice 94, which has notes of warm allspice, cardamom, and citrus, and lingering bittersweet qualities that make for a delightful concentrate in earthy, non-alcoholic cocktails.

THE BARTENDER'S PANTRY

The bartender's pantry is a real mix. It looks part apothecary (with the little bottles of bitters and tinctures), part baker's cupboard (with the sugars, sugar alternatives, and vinegars), and part teahouse (with the dried teas, kombuchas, and tonics). However, for your home bar to be fully functioning, I can't recommend enough having access to at least something from each category. By doing so, you'll be able to create *your* version of every cocktail in this book!

Sugars and Sugar Alternatives

Sugar content is integral to making cocktails. With so many variations of sweeteners and about a few thousand ways to use them, I'm providing you with a quick snapshot of what is available to you. Sugar levels are usually measured in Brix, which refers to the percentage of sugar that is dissolved in water. You will see on the next pages that you can't simply substitute one sugar source for another. As an example, honey, which I love to use to infuse drinks with a deeply sweetened flavor, exists in the range of 70–88 Brix. Simple syrup (made from dissolving granular sugar in water), on the other hand, is only 50 Brix. So, you need to know your sugars!

1 White Sugar

We are all familiar with white granulated sugar, which is made from sugarcane that is milled and boiled to separate the juices until it crystalizes. In this process, the molasses and impurities are removed to give the sugar its pure white coloration. This type of sugar is great for creating simple syrups that will take on any flavor without adding too much sweetness.

2 Demerara

Demerara is a raw sugar extracted directly from sugarcane and minimally processed, leaving medium to coarse crystals that still have a bit of molasses. Demerara's hint of smokiness, light bitterness, and spice yields more depth of flavor in cocktails. Add it to a Mojito and immediately it will enhance the flavors of an aged rum.

3 Honey

Honey starts as a nectar from flowers collected by honeybees. The nectar gets broken down into simple sugars inside the honeycomb, and then evaporates over time to create liquid honey. The difference in color and flavor comes from the plants the bees choose to collect the nectar from, and oh boy is there a difference! I personally only go for all-natural raw honey. If you get your hands on some really special stuff like the Lignum Mango Blossom Honey collected by the honeybees from the blossoms of mango trees grown in Jamaica, you are in for a treat! This honey has tropical notes, warm tones, and a pleasing floral nature that is happy in almost any cocktail.

4 Maple Syrup

As a Canadian, I love using maple syrup. The concentrate made from the sap of a sugar maple tree (which contains about 98 percent water and 2 percent sugar) is typically around 66 Brix—which, incidentally, is when it can officially be called a maple syrup. One gallon of maple syrup can be made by using about 40 gallons of sap. So, if you didn't know why this Canadian staple will set you back a lot of loonies, now you do! However, I think the cost is always worth it, as maple syrup adds a rich, earthy tone to cocktails that is hard to replicate.

Agave Nectar

This alternative is derived from a few species of the succulent that's famous for giving us tequilas and mezcals. When you find a premium-quality agave nectar, it yields a subtle, smoky flavor and sits around 65–79 Brix. However, buyer beware! Check the label to make sure your agave nectar hasn't been cut with high-fructose corn syrup.

Other Mixers, Acidifiers, and Lengtheners

Here are some other items that will truly round out your home bar pantry. Although not every category is completely needed, it will enhance your drink-making experience dramatically if you have the items listed. If you are just beginning, I recommend you start small with quality items and slowly build up to brands and expressions you like. Each one of these categories has enough selection that I could dedicate an entire chapter to each of them. So, have fun—run wild!

⑤ Bitters and Tinctures

A form of concentrate that is like salt to any plated food, bitters and tinctures serve to enhance the flavors of the other ingredients in your cocktail by either complementing or contrasting them. Tinctures are generally concentrated flavorings, whereas bitters contain, well, bittering agents. Angostura, a Trinidadian bitters used in a plethora of classic cocktails, and which is easily sourced, is a home bar staple. (Historically it was a medicinal digestion aid!) There are many other bitters you will see in this book, but having a classic Angostura Trinidadian bitters on hand is a must.

⑥ Frothing Agent

If you're into sours and frothy drinks, the best way to achieve that texture is by using egg whites. One ounce of pasteurized egg whites equals roughly one egg. In the act of shaking a sour cocktail, the aeration causes the protein from the egg white to froth, creating the fluffy texture that is so popular in cocktails such as the Whiskey Sour. Egg whites, however, do not add flavor, just texture—and they are 100 percent safe to use! Recently some vegan alternatives have come on the market and my go-to is Ms. Better's Bitters Miraculous Foamer. A mere five or six drops of this substitute will achieve the desired frothiness cocktail lovers want. It is less stable after time in the glass, but your cocktail will be so delicious that it probably won't matter.

⑦ Acidifiers

Vinegars are a great way to acidify anything, and they can also add flavor. There is a huge difference between the styles of vinegars out there, but I generally use a quality raw apple cider vinegar as it carries more than just tartness. Drinking vinegars are commonly known as "shrubs."

Alternative acidifiers come in the form of citric and malic acid. Citric acid is commonly and naturally found in lemons and limes, while malic acid is found in other fruits and vegetables like oranges, apples, grapes, and tomatoes. Malic acid carries a slightly softer acidity. I often use both as preservatives for some of the syrups I make, which can add depth to a cocktail without volume.

⑧ Dried Things

Salts and dried herbs and spices are ways to, literally, spice up your drinks without adding volume. These items will take your ordinary cocktails to the next level by adding a touch of concentrated flavor, while also helping to highlight the rest of the ingredients in your drink. My go-tos are Maldon salt for syrup preparations and kosher salt for rimming a glass. I always make sure to have fennel seeds, cloves, and cinnamon on hand as they complement and enhance a range of flavor profiles, from gin to whiskies.

Teas are incredible carriers of flavors that range from bright and fruity to smoky and tannic. For cocktails they are some of the quickest infusions you can create, and they also offer the widest range of flavors that are shelf stable and accessible. I recommend having at least an herbal, a green, and a black tea on hand that you love. Tea is also a great lengthener for non-alcoholic drinks.

Kombuchas and Tepache

If you want fun, funky flavors, consider adding these fermented beverages to your mix. Kombuchas are typically lightly effervescent and are made from fermenting sugared black or green teas using a SCOBY (symbiotic culture of bacteria and yeasts)—hot tip, this is also what makes kimchi so damned good!

Kombuchas can be flavored with fruit, herbs, or spices, and add an interesting, soft depth to a cocktail, especially in non-alcoholic servings. (Do beware of the possible alcohol content that could result from long periods of fermentation.) Tepache dates back to pre-Columbian Mexico, and is a delicious, fermented pineapple beverage from the peels and rinds of the fruit. It can be flavored with spices, depending on your taste, and often carries notes of baking spice, earthiness, and, of course, tropical fruit. Easily replicable at home (see my recipe on page 204), this is a great drink to have on its own or mixed with agave spirits.

Quality Sparkling Water and Tonics

If you're going to make good drinks, you should really start with good products. Premium tonics are a must when it comes to making a Gin and Tonic, but are also a fantastic add-on for some quinine flavor in a tall cocktail that needs lengthening. Sparkling water acts as an agent for dilution but also adds texture to the beverage from long to large-format drinks. I tend to use a home carbonation machine so my drinks don't carry any extra minerality or salinity—unless, of course, that's what you are going for.

COCKTAILS FOR EVERY MOOD

I truly believe that the enjoyment of cocktails is dictated by the time, space, and company you keep. As I write this passage at 8:00 p.m. on a Wednesday, I'm loving my gin Martini; but on a Saturday afternoon with friends, chances are I'll feel a bit more adventurous and might like a tiki-style punch. I have organized the following chapters to suit any occasion and any mood you may be in. Dig in, enjoy. There should be something in here for any day, any time, and anyone.

The Four Keys to Professional Quality Cocktails at Home

Ice

Understanding the why behind cooling and diluting your cocktails is like understanding how fire affects your food. Whether you are drinking a dram on the rocks or shaking up a Daiquiri, dilution is the key to all cocktails (as it is for hot water and Hot Toddies). An ample amount of ice allows your cocktails to chill while diluting them, so the abundance of mixed liquids becomes a whole. When ice is used properly, your cocktail will move one step closer from good to great. And trust me, you're going to need a lot of ice—way more than you can imagine. So set up a system and get shaking! Or stirring!

SHAKEN OR STIRRED?

The ever-so-famous question. Both are methods to help you achieve the goal of making room-temperature liquids cold enough that they're enjoyable to drink. So why does James Bond prefer his Vesper Martini shaken? Truthfully, no one knows. What I do know is, as a general rule, cocktails containing a good amount of citrus are better served shaken. Shaking with ice provides the drink with aeration, which is a fancy word for the integration of micro-bubbles into the liquid solution. By shaking vigorously, those bubbles provide the drink with great frothy texture that makes the acidity from the citrus pop. When shaking a cocktail, it is best to fill your shaking vessel with enough ice to cover the liquid, plus a bit more, so the liquid sits three quarters of the way up the ice. Shake your drink in a back-and-forth motion, ensuring that the ice hits the top and the bottom of your mixing vessel. Lastly, strain out your liquid (using a Hawthorne strainer if you have one) so it holds the spent or old ice back—those cubes have done their job!

Stirring is a more delicate way of chilling a cocktail. Generally, cocktails that are spirit forward, and for which you don't want much dilution (like a Martini, a Negroni, or an Old Fashioned) are the kind you'll want to stir as aeration often doesn't do this kind of cocktail any favors. Instead, stirring the drink in a mixing glass with a bar spoon, in a smooth and swift motion, delicately chills and dilutes the liquid. This preserves the beautiful notes of your base spirit while maintaining the viscous, velvety texture a drink should have. As with a shaken cocktail, I prefer to toss the spent ice and introduce new ice to the cocktail in the serving glass, if it is called for on the rocks.

Measure Everything

One of the biggest lessons I have learned through creating and making cocktails is the difficulty of balance. If you are wondering why your cocktails sometimes just aren't right, it's because you have started in a place where you were already off-center—likely by not measuring your base ingredient. Measuring everything, including your base ingredient, will set you up for a solid foundation for adding the rest of the supporting ingredients. It also enables you to figure out where your preferences lie, so, when it does come time to get creative, you'll know how much of what to add to suit your palate! (It also means you can guide bartenders toward your flavor preferences when out at the bar—politely, of course!)

The only bar tool you need for this is a jigger—the bartender's measuring cup. If you don't have one, here is an easy measurement conversion chart:

> ½ oz = 15 ml = 1 tablespoon
> 1 oz = 30 ml = 2 tablespoons
> 2 oz = 60 ml = 4 tablespoons

You will find this chart helpful because (surprise!) you're about to do some measuring.

Don't Over Complicate Things

While you may see a couple of "complex" syrups and shrubs in this book, I promise you that making them will be well worth it. The fact is that sometimes a four-ingredient cocktail featuring a shrub (or a tincture or a syrup) will deliver a much more complex and put-together experience than a seven-ingredient drink without one. Not all the time, but most times. People create liqueurs, tinctures, and shrubs for a reason.

And don't be afraid of simplicity. A drink doesn't need a bunch of *za-za zoom* ingredients to make it great. What it needs is careful and deliberate consideration for the flavors that are meant to be pulled or highlighted from the initial pour of the base ingredient. Don't think too hard on it, let the ingredients speak for themselves.

Garnish Purposefully

We enjoy drinks in terms of taste, smell, *and* looks. And a good garnish is the cherry on top of a beautifully diluted and composed cocktail. (Sometimes, it's an actual cherry!) However, an overcomplicated garnish can do more harm than good. Garnishes should enhance the flavors of the cocktail by either highlighting the existing notes with complementary ones, or contrasting them with opposite ones—like a sweet with a sour. Doing so will enable you to reach exciting crescendos in your imbibing journey. Later in the book you will find easy but purposeful garnish suggestions that will very much enhance your drinking experiences.

EASY-PEASY FANCY GARNISHES

You drink with your eyes as much as you drink with your nose and palate. These garnishes seem a bit fancy, but they are a fantastic way to introduce some extra flavor and aromatics to your base drink. They can also tie together your finished beverage in a beautiful and meaningful way. Sometimes all you need is a bit of citrus oil to really brighten up a drink.

Dehydrated Citrus Wheel

This is an easy way to garnish a cocktail so it smells like the concentrated and caramelized sugars of the citrus fruit. It also looks pretty and is shelf stable, so you can make a bunch of these and you are set. To make, place citrus on a cutting board and use a sharp knife to cut off the top and bottom. Place the citrus on its side and slice to create wheels. Make each wheel about ¼ inch thick. Put citrus wheels on a cooking rack on a baking sheet and put in the oven at 200°F. Leave for at least 4–6 hours, flipping once. Occasionally check on the wheels to ensure they don't burn. Alternatively, if you have a dehydrator, set it to 150°F and dehydrate for about 4–6 hours.

Candied Citrus

An edible garnish that is fantastic on crushed ice to add dynamic colors as well as some delicious fruit flavors. To make, place citrus on a cutting board and use a sharp knife to cut the top and bottom off the citrus. Cut citrus into wheels about ¼ inch thick. To a sterilized mason jar, add 1 teaspoon of white granulated sugar to cover the bottom. Add 1 wheel and add another teaspoon of sugar to cover. Repeat the process with all the wheels, with the last layer being sugar to cover the citrus. Using a piece of plastic wrap, press down firmly on the citrus stack and cover. Leave at room temperature for 12 hours until fruit is soft and sugars have slightly dissolved. Store in the refrigerator for up to 3 weeks. I tend to use cara cara oranges for their combination of floral and sweet notes.

Citrus Flower

Take a whole citrus (lemons, oranges, and grapefruits are best) and use a potato peeler to go around the circumference and peel off a long strip of zest. As if making a fruit roll-up, start from one end and slowly roll the peel into itself. Anchor the end through the middle of the "flower" with a cocktail pick. This garnish can seem slightly aggressive, but is large enough to garnish an extravagant tiki drink or a cocktail served in a large glass.

Citrus Square

This garnish is the simplest way to introduce extra aromatics to a stirred cocktail. Using your potato peeler, simply take a wide strip of peel off your citrus. Trim to make a square (and save the rest of the peel for the Easy Citrus Peel Cordial on page 192!). Hold it by its edges with the outside of the peel (the oily side) facing the drink and lightly squeeze to release oils. Drop it in the drink and serve!

Citrus Twist

With a potato peeler, take off a wide strip of citrus peel, about 2 inches long. Trim lengthwise down both sides to cut the uneven peel off. You should now have a rectangle with uneven ends. Take an end and cut it on a 30-degree angle, perpendicular to the side. Rotate the peel 180 degrees and cut the other end off on the same 30-degree angle. Hold the peel on its ends and twist it over your drink, making a slight coil. The sweet oils will release into the drink as you twist. Drop it in the drink and serve. A navel orange is my citrus of choice as the skins contain bittersweet oils with a ton of brightness.

Citrus Ribbon

With a potato peeler, peel off a strip from your citrus that is at least 2 inches long. Use a sharp knife and trim down both sides, so the ends form a tip, sort of in the shape of a surfboard. Score a sliver lengthwise down the middle of the peel without cutting the peel in half. Fold one end of the peel inwards, keeping the oily side facing outward, and tuck it in the sliver. Repeat on the other end. Set the ribbon on the rim of a cocktail served up. This garnish is perfect for providing aromatics without the oils actually going into the drink.

Cucumber Ribbon

Run your potato peeler lengthwise down an entire cucumber and remove the very top skin. Repeat the process again so you have a long strip with skin on the edges and flesh in the middle. As if you are making a fruit roll-up, start from one end and slowly roll the strip into itself. Stop 1/8 of the way down the strip. Take a cocktail skewer and skewer through the middle of the roll to anchor it. Fold the rest of the cucumber strip back and forth into the skewer, making an accordion or wave-like appearance. Do this until the strip is completely secured by the skewer. This edible garnish is great with cocktails that include my Cucumber Lime Cordial.

Apple Fan

On a cutting board, stand an apple upright. Take a sharp knife and slice off one side of the apple from top to bottom, about 1/8 inch away from the core. Set rest of the apple aside. Lay the piece you cut off flesh side down on the cutting board. Trim a 1/2-inch piece off the left and right edges so the flesh is showing, not peel, and discard (or eat!). Thinly slice the apple lengthwise, keeping the slices side by side. Use a cocktail pick and skewer through the middle-bottom to hold the slices together. Proceed to fan out the slices and place gently on the side of a glass. This can also be done with pears.

Herb-Berry Skewer

The herbs and berries are interchangeable for this garnish. The point is that you use your herb stem as the fruit skewer. In this example I'm using a rosemary sprig and raspberries. Remove the leaves off 3/4 of the rosemary stem, starting from the bottom, leaving the top 1/4 of the leaves intact. Take raspberries and use the stem to skewer through the berries. Place the skewer into a tall drink vertically or lay it over a coupe glass for a short drink garnish.

GENERAL RECIPE NOTES

- Ice is featured in nearly every cocktail recipe in this book. Its role is to cool and dilute your beverage. Certain methods of creation call for more ice than others. While ice may not be listed as an ingredient in the recipes, you should assume that you need ice, and lots of it.

- Juices from citrus are always best when fresh. Juices from other fruit may be canned, bottled, or fresh, but generally, find the least processed expression of whatever juice you need to use.

- Garnishes are optional. But remember that they can enhance your cocktail experience in a significant way—if it is called for in the recipe, then it is generally preferred that you include it. However, if you feel like a garnish might break the bank, or if you simply don't have time to include it—no sweat. What's most important is that what you put in the glass is measured, balanced, and delicious.

- Tea-making is always best done by following the tea producer's instructions. That's what I do. Unless it is a strongly steeped tea the recipe calls for. In which case follow my instructions!

- Glassware is important, so be sure to follow the glassware guide in this book (see page 12). But if you don't have the right stuff, just find a vessel that is of a similar size and shape.

COOL AS A CUCUMBER

Providing a collection of insanely fresh drinks that will cool you down on the hottest days of the summer, as well as those that are simply delightful and easy to approach as an aperitif, this chapter is seriously refreshing. Ranging from simple highballs and shaken cocktails with fruit to in-depth tiki drinks, there is something in here for everyone—even those who identify as staunch lovers of their whiskey neat! Enjoy!

IN THIS CHAPTER...

Miso Bees-ies

Fermented soybeans in a cocktail? Damn straight! I love using miso in cooking so I started experimenting with this umami flavoring in cocktails. Turns out, it's terrific! This drink is a take on a classic Bee's Knees with the addition of white miso paste for an earthy, salty-sweet, and floral character. Made with a New Western Dry Gin, you'll also find notes of lavender and citrus.

½ bar spoon (¼ Tbsp) white miso paste

1 oz lemon juice

¾ oz Best Base Honey Syrup (see page 186)

2 oz Aviation Gin

1   In a cocktail shaker, combine miso paste, lemon juice, and syrup.

2   Use a bar spoon to whisk until well integrated, forming a paste.

3   Add gin.

4   Add enough ice to cover the liquid in the shaker, plus a bit more.

5   Cover and shake vigorously for 10–15 seconds.

6   Strain through a Hawthorne strainer into a 5-oz coupe glass. No garnish needed.

Green Awakening

During the COVID-19 lockdown I got really into using the leftover tops and bottoms of fruit to make syrups for my cocktails. This recipe features my scrap-based Cucumber Lime Cordial. The cocktail combines a Junmai sake with Hendrick's Gin carrying floral notes of rose, cucumbers, and tart green apples. It's a green-on-green celebration!

1 oz Junmai sake

1 oz Hendrick's Gin

¾ oz Cucumber Lime Cordial (see page 193)

½ oz green apple juice

¼ oz lime juice

Rinse of absinthe

Cucumber ribbon, for garnish (see page 49)

1   Chill a 7-oz coupe glass in the freezer.

2   In a cocktail shaker, combine all ingredients but the absinthe and cucumber ribbon.

3   Add enough ice to cover the liquid in the shaker, plus a bit more.

4   Cover and shake vigorously for 10–15 seconds.

5   Rinse your chilled coupe glass with absinthe.

6   Strain cocktail through a Hawthorne strainer into the chilled coupe glass.

7   Garnish with the cucumber ribbon on a skewer.

Green Awakening, p. 56 and Not Your Typical Lychee Martini, p. 58

Not Your Typical Lychee Martini

I love 1990s nostalgia, so what better way to relive the Doc Martens, neoprene jackets, and crop tops than a Lychee Martini? Unfortunately, this cocktail is often made with lots of artificial sweetener, and that sucks. So, instead, here's a version that's as sweet and sassy as *Melrose Place* without the guilt, featuring homemade Lychee Lime Cordial.

1 oz Spanish dry vermouth

1 oz Dillon's Rose Gin

½ oz Lychee Lime Cordial (see Tip)

¼ oz St-Germain Elderflower Liqueur

Lemon twist, for garnish (see page 48)

1 In a cocktail shaker, combine all ingredients but the lemon twist.

2 Add enough ice to cover the liquid in the shaker, plus a bit more.

3 Cover and shake vigorously for 10–15 seconds.

4 Strain through a Hawthorne strainer into a 7-oz coupe glass.

5 Garnish with the lemon twist.

TIP

To make Lychee Lime Cordial, use the Cucumber Lime Cordial recipe on page 193, but substitute lychee juice for the cucumber juice.

Pink Tuxedo

I've always wanted a tuxedo, and if I were to get one, I imagine it would be bad ass—the body made of pink silk and framed by a dark lapel. This bold and flavorful number is the cocktail equivalent of my dream tux. It is an amazing variation on a sour with a frothy texture and made with a tart, earthy, and vibrant Rhubarb Saffron Shrub.

1½ oz Collective Arts Rhubarb & Hibiscus Gin*

¼ oz Aperol

¾ oz Rhubarb Saffron Shrub (see page 195)

1 egg white

Rhubarb stalk, peeled and curled, for garnish (see Tip)

The Collective Arts gin used here adds an extra rhubarb kick, but you can substitute with any dry gin featuring floral botanicals.

1   In a cocktail shaker, combine all ingredients but the rhubarb stalk.

2   Cover and shake without ice to aerate the drink and create a bit of frothiness.

3   Add enough ice to cover the liquid in the shaker, plus a bit more.

4   Cover and shake vigorously for 10–15 seconds.

5   Strain through a Hawthorne strainer into a 7-oz coupe glass.

6   Garnish with the strip of curled rhubarb and secure it to the glass with a small clip or a cocktail pick.

> **TIP**
>
> To make a curled rhubarb stalk, place a single stalk of rhubarb, ribbed side up, on a cutting board. Take a potato peeler and peel lengthwise, discarding the top pieces. Repeat until you have a long smooth strip you can twist into itself and secure with a cocktail pick (see picture on page 115).

Apple 'n' Herbs

Apples, spruce, and pine are very much in abundance in Canada, and who knew that they make one of those delightful pairings that yields a delicious Gimlet-style cocktail? (Especially when used with vodka distilled from Canadian milk sugar!) This is going to be a fan favorite for your pre-dinner get-togethers.

2 oz Vodkow Vodka

3/4 oz cloudy apple juice

1/2 oz Chamomile and Meyer Lemon Syrup (see page 187)

3/4 oz lime juice

4 dashes Pine and Spruce Tincture (see page 198)

Red apple fan, for garnish (see page 49)

1 In a cocktail shaker, combine all ingredients but the red apple fan.

2 Add enough ice to cover the liquid in the shaker, plus a bit more.

3 Cover and shake vigorously for 10–15 seconds.

4 Strain through a Hawthorne strainer into an 8-oz coupe glass.

5 Garnish with the red apple fan.

Garden Party

Like a brilliant garden party, this drink of herbs, roots, and fruits celebrates summer and aims to capture that special time when farmers' markets are in full swing. The market in my neighborhood, at Trinity Bellwoods Park, is an excellent example of Canadian agriculture bringing people together from all walks of life. I made this cocktail based on the sights and scents found at the market.

1 oz Spirit of York Gin

½ oz sloe gin (see Tip)

½ oz Amaro Montenegro

½ oz Easy Citrus Peel Cordial (see page 192)

¾ oz lemon juice

3 drops Bittered Sling Suius Cherry Bitters

Edible flower, for garnish (optional)

1   In a cocktail shaker, combine all ingredients but the edible flower.

2   Add enough ice to cover the liquid in the shaker, plus a bit more.

3   Cover and shake vigorously for 10–15 seconds.

4   Strain through a Hawthorne strainer into a 7-oz coupe glass.

5   Garnish with an edible flower (optional).

I love supporting Canadian creators, and Bittered Sling is a fantastic bitters producer out of British Columbia. Their suius cherry bitters blends Lapins cherries from BC's Okanagan Valley with a unique combination of herbs, spices, roots, and barks. With flavors of gentian, American oak, and anise-family botanicals, this expression is a great grab for southern-style aromatic bitters.

TIP

Sloe gin is a dazzlingly red gin expression made from the addition of sloe berries (a cousin of the plum). It is lower in ABV than gin, and adds a slight fruit note to a cocktail. It can be used as a base spirit or as an additive.

Fig Dreams

I love to fuel my body first thing in the morning with a nice bowl of yogurt and fruit. And that's the inspiration for this low-ABV cocktail that carries dreamy fruit flavors, notes of honeysuckle, gentian, and herbs, and a dairy-like creaminess. Dare I say this cocktail is breakfast ready?

1½ oz Fig and Black Pepper Infused Cocchi Americano (see page 200)

¼ oz Yellow Chartreuse

½ oz lemon juice

½ oz Best Base Honey Syrup (see page 186)

1½ Tbsp dairy-free yogurt

Fresh fig, cut in half, for garnish

1 In a cocktail shaker, combine all ingredients but the fresh fig.

2 Cover and shake without ice to break down the yogurt.

3 Add enough ice to cover the liquid in the shaker, plus a bit more.

4 Cover and shake vigorously for 10–15 seconds.

5 Pour contents of the shaker into a Collins glass and top with more ice.

6 Garnish with the fresh fig.

Calm Seas

When in a seaside town, one of my favorite moments of the day is sitting at the edge of a dock and taking in the calmness of the sea in the morning. Designed for my nautical friends who share my love of the ocean, this worldly cocktail contains salinity and earthy tones balanced with the fresh and grassy backbone of cachaça and Fino Sherry.

1½ oz Nori Infused Fino Sherry (see page 199)

½ oz cachaça

½ oz Easy Rich Syrup (see page 184)

¼ oz Islay Scotch

¾ oz lime juice

1 piece nori, cut to 1½ x 2 inches, for garnish

1   In a cocktail shaker, combine all ingredients but the nori.

2   Add enough ice to cover the liquid in the shaker, plus a bit more.

3   Cover and shake vigorously for 10–15 seconds.

4   Strain through a Hawthorne strainer into a 10-oz Collins glass filled with ice.

5   Garnish with the piece of nori, tucked lengthwise into the side of the glass (the ice will hold it up).

Big Pony Swizzle

This delicious, tropical-forward cocktail is inspired by my father's love of horse racing, cigars, and desserts. This is a fun swizzle with toastiness from the orgeat and hints of honey, orange, and vanilla from the amaro, along with some added caramel and tropical flavors.

1½ oz Sailor Jerry Spiced Rum

½ oz Amaro Nonino

½ oz Cashew Orgeat (see page 186)

1 oz pineapple juice

¾ oz lime juice

2 dashes absinthe

4 dashes Angostura Bitters

Pineapple fronds, for garnish

Fresh lime wheel, for garnish

1 In a tall 14-oz Collins or tiki glass, combine all ingredients but the pineapple fronds and lime wheel.

2 Fill the glass with ice.

3 Insert a bar spoon into the middle of the glass until it reaches the bottom.

4 Put the handle of the bar spoon between your palms and, in a back-and-forth fashion (like you are trying to warm your hands), "swizzle" the cocktail, agitating the liquid and ice with the motion created from your spoon. Do this for 5-10 seconds, until cocktail is chilled.

5 Fill glass with more ice and garnish with pineapple fronds and the lime wheel.

Tropical Secrets

I want you to picture yourself in Mexico. Think of yourself sitting elegantly on a beach chair watching the waves—not partying hardy in Cancun. This drink is meant to be a tropical paradise in a glass. (However, if your paradise is the resort pool in Cancun, that works! No judgement here!) This tequila cocktail is essentially a play on a deconstructed Pina Colada and is sure to be a fan favorite—no matter the locale.

1½ oz Tequila Tromba Reposado

½ oz Coconut Infused Amontillado Sherry (see page 199)

½ oz Caramelized Banana Peel Rich Syrup (see page 185)

¾ oz lime juice

3 oz tepache (see page 204)

Toasted coconut flakes, for garnish (optional)

1 In a cocktail shaker, combine all ingredients but the tepache.

2 Add enough ice to cover the liquid in the shaker, plus a bit more.

3 Cover and shake vigorously for 10–15 seconds.

4 Strain through a Hawthorne strainer into a 12-oz Collins glass.

5 Add ice and top with tepache. Stir to integrate flavors.

6 Garnish with toasted coconut flakes (optional).

Queen Cobbler, p. 74 and Nutty Doctor, p. 75

Queen Cobbler

I love to dream about traveling in Spain, but for now I'll have to settle for indulging in the sumptuous flavors of the region. This low-ABV cocktail is loaded with notes of almonds, figs, Meyer lemons, and herbs. This drink also stands as my ode to the Sherry Cobbler—the cocktail that changed my perception of Sherry from being overly sweet and belonging in the back of a liquor cabinet to "This is the best thing that has ever happened to me!"

¼ lemon, cut into small wedges

¼ orange, cut into small wedges

½ oz Chamomile and Meyer Lemon Syrup (see page 187)

1½ oz Oloroso Sherry

1½ oz Amontillado Sherry

Fresh orange slice, for garnish

Mint sprig, for garnish

1   In a cocktail shaker, combine lemon wedges, orange wedges, and syrup. Muddle until juices are released and fruits are broken down.

2   Add both Sherries.

3   Add enough ice to cover the liquid in the shaker, plus a bit more.

4   Cover and shake vigorously for 10–15 seconds.

5   Strain through a Hawthorne strainer into a 13-oz wine glass. Fill with cracked ice and garnish with the orange slice and mint sprig.

> **TIP**
>
> Feel free to add 2 additional tablespoons of fruit to this cocktail in step 1. Stone fruit, like peaches and nectarines, will bring out more of the nutty notes of the Sherry. Berries, like blackberries and raspberries, will work to highlight the citrus and floral qualities of the Sherry.

Nutty Doctor

One of the most intriguing distillery tours I have experienced was going to the Hiram Walker & Sons Distillery in Windsor, Ontario, where Wiser's and Lot No. 40 are produced. There I met Dr. Don, who presented the flavor wheel of Canadian whisky that showed, among other things, that these whiskies are highly versatile and compatible with many flavors you might not necessarily think of. This tropical and unusual whisky cocktail is an ode to Dr. Don!

1½ oz Lot No. 40 100% Pot Still Rye Whisky

½ oz Coconut Infused Amontillado Sherry (see page 199)

¾ oz Cashew Orgeat (see page 186)

¾ oz lemon juice

2 dashes Bittered Sling Moondog Latin Bitters

Large toasted coconut flakes, for garnish

Mint sprig, for garnish

1   In a cocktail shaker, combine all ingredients but the toasted coconut and mint sprig.

2   Add enough ice to cover the liquid in the shaker, plus a bit more.

3   Cover and shake vigorously for 10–15 seconds.

4   Pour contents of shaker into a 12-oz rocks glass and top with cracked ice.

5   Garnish with the large flakes of toasted coconut and mint sprig.

Purple Dreams

I often find inspiration for unique cocktails in distant memories of my motherland, Hong Kong. There I had a caretaker named Wilma, and she used to make halo-halo (shaved ice) with ube (purple yam) ice cream for me and my sister. I still crave those flavors. This cocktail hints at those fun, nostalgic memories, and is vibrant, unique, and full of life—much like the Asian community.

1 oz Bacardi Coconut Rum

1 oz cachaça

½ oz Ube Rich Syrup (see page 185)

¾ oz Acid Adjusted Pineapple Juice (see page 195)

Fresh lime wheel, for garnish

Pineapple fronds, for garnish

1   In a cocktail shaker, add all ingredients but the lime wheel and pineapple fronds.

2   Add enough ice to cover the liquid in the shaker, plus a bit more.

3   Cover and shake vigorously for 10–15 seconds.

4   Pour contents of shaker into a 12-oz rocks glass and top with cracked ice.

5   Garnish the side of the glass with the lime wheel and pineapple fronds.

Sweet Tea Sundays

Inspired by southern hospitality and my first trip to the Kentucky Bourbon Trail, this silly, simple, boozy "sweet tea" can be made well ahead of time in batches to entertain friends. The chai syrup brings out some of those delightful baking spice notes found in Kentucky bourbon. Be careful, though. This one is dangerously good!

1½ oz Angel's Envy Bourbon

½ oz Amontillado Sherry

¾ oz lemon juice

½ oz Chai Rich Syrup (see page 184)

4 dashes Bittered Sling Clingstone Peach Bitters

Dehydrated lemon wheel, for garnish (see page 48)

Peach wedge, for garnish

1 In a cocktail shaker, combine all ingredients but the dehydrated lemon wheel and peach wedge.

2 Add enough ice to cover the liquid in the shaker, plus a bit more.

3 Cover and shake vigorously for 10–15 seconds.

4 Pour contents into a 12-oz rocks glass and top with more ice.

5 Garnish with the dehydrated lemon wheel and peach wedge.

Mama Rosa

During my travels in Oaxaca, Mexico, the small family-run mezcalarias were often my favorite places to stop. The caretaker of the family, most often the mother or grandmother, would be making fresh tortillas in the back while proudly displaying their family's land and offerings to their guests. This "all things pink" cocktail is smoky, fruit forward, and filled with warmth and earthiness, and is dedicated to the mamas of the house. The hibiscus and pink peppercorn flavors provide a burst of tartness that also carries an incredible floral punch.

$1\frac{1}{2}$ oz espadin mezcal

$\frac{1}{2}$ oz Martini Riserva Speciale Bitter

$\frac{1}{2}$ oz Hibiscus and Pink Peppercorn Rich Syrup (see page 185)

$\frac{3}{4}$ oz Acid Adjusted Grapefruit Juice (see page 195)

2 drops Saline Solution (see page 203)

Long grapefruit twist, for garnish (see page 48)

1. In a cocktail shaker, combine all ingredients but the grapefruit twist.

2. Add enough ice to cover the liquid in the shaker, plus a bit more.

3. Cover and shake vigorously for 10–15 seconds.

4. Strain through a Hawthorne strainer into an 8-oz coupe glass.

5. Garnish with the grapefruit twist.

S'up Wit Dat?

A vibrant blend of intriguing flavors inspired by my trips to Oaxaca in southwestern Mexico, this cocktail is a modified version of one of the famed cocktails I made for an experimental cocktail bar I helped create. Loaded with herbal and smoky qualities that are balanced by the freshness of cucumbers and pine, the guests you serve this to will be happily asking you, "S'up wit dat?"

1½ oz Sombra Mezcal

½ oz Spanish dry vermouth

¾ oz Cucumber Lime Cordial (see page 193)

½ oz lime juice

4 dashes Pine and Spruce Tincture (see page 198)

3 drops Saline Solution (see page 203)

Cucumber ribbon, for garnish (see page 49)

1 In a cocktail shaker, combine all ingredients but the cucumber ribbon.

2 Add enough ice to cover the liquid in the shaker, plus a bit more.

3 Cover and shake vigorously for 10–15 seconds.

4 Strain through a Hawthorne strainer into a 12-oz rocks glass over fresh ice cubes.

5 Garnish with the cucumber ribbon.

Dr. Somebody

My mother comes from a large family, and I always enjoyed the stories told by my uncle, who was an ER doctor. I remember the meals, the conversations, and his intense love of Scotch and tong sui to decompress after a long day at work. Tong sui is a delicate, sweet, and floral Chinese dessert made with snow fungus, red dates, goji berries, and rock sugar (once in a while there may be a pear in it as well). This cocktail is designed for him. And for the memory of when I thought I'd strive to be a doctor, too—and thereby, maybe one day, a somebody!

¼ Asian pear, cut into small cubes

1 oz Glenlivet Founder's Reserve Scotch

1 oz Lillet Blanc

¼ oz Easy Rich Syrup (see page 184)

¾ oz lemon juice

Pear fan, for garnish (see page 49)

1 In a cocktail shaker, muddle Asian pear to release juices, then add in all ingredients but the pear fan.

2 Add enough ice to cover the liquid in the shaker, plus a bit more.

3 Cover and shake vigorously for 10–15 seconds.

4 Strain through a Hawthorne strainer into a 12-oz rocks glass over fresh ice cubes.

5 Garnish with the pear fan.

White Peaks

I once worked at a fine dining restaurant in Vancouver, the Blue Water Cafe, where I truly learned the meaning of "finesse" in food service. White linen, an extensive wine cellar, a massive back bar with a plethora of Scotches, spirits, wines, and sakes, and a team of exacting sushi chefs who created exquisitely assembled dishes. This simple cocktail is an ode to finesse and to the chefs at the Blue Water who understood the nuances of flavor, even if they weren't familiar with cocktails on their own.

1½ oz nigori sake

¾ oz Plymouth Gin

½ oz Mugicha Rich Syrup (see page 185)

¾ oz lemon juice

Candied ginger, for garnish

Lemon twist, for garnish (see page 48)

1 In a cocktail shaker, combine all ingredients but the candied ginger and lemon twist.

2 Add enough ice to cover the liquid in the shaker, plus a bit more.

3 Cover and shake vigorously for 10–15 seconds.

4 Strain through a Hawthorne strainer into a 12-oz rocks glass over fresh ice.

5 Garnish with the candied ginger and lemon twist.

Nigori, meaning "cloudy," is an unfiltered sake containing remnants of rice solids that are not fermented. This imparts a creamy texture and some rustic qualities to the sake, making it a fabulous low-ABV cocktail ingredient. Make sure to give the bottle a shake to integrate the sediment before pouring.

The Easy Pea-sy Rickey

I love a good Gin Rickey—typically spirit, citrus, and soda. I've created this drink to highlight a relatively new entrant to the cocktail game: snap peas! With some vegetal notes and mild sweetness, the peas pair well with gin that is heavy on evergreen botanicals. Time to give this underrated vegetable some hype!

3 sugar snap peas (2 peas cut into pieces, 1 pea for garnish)

1 oz St. George Terroir Gin

¼ oz Green Chartreuse

½ oz lime juice

1 bar spoon (½ Tbsp) Easy Rich Syrup (see page 184)

2 oz sparkling water

1 In a cocktail shaker, smash and muddle the chopped snap peas until broken down, then add gin, Chartreuse, lime juice, and syrup.

2 Add enough ice to cover the liquid in the shaker, plus a bit more.

3 Cover and shake vigorously for 10–15 seconds.

4 Strain through a fine cone strainer into a 10-oz Collins glass and fill with ice.

5 Add sparkling water and stir with a bar spoon.

6 Garnish with the whole sugar snap pea.

Cynar Paloma

The Paloma is a classic: tequila accented with puckering acid from lime and grapefruit and topped off with the refreshing zip of bright bubbles. It is a refreshing alternative to the sometimes too-sweet Margarita. But, me? I love a twist or two, you might say. So, for a daringly bitter alternative that I think is the perfect summer digestif, try this recipe on for size. Alongside the traditional grapefruit notes, this Paloma will transport you to a place you never thought possible with hints of caramel, coffee, and cinnamon.

1 tsp Love of Cocktails Grapefruit and Pink Peppercorn Salt Rimmer*

1 lime wedge

1 oz Patron Silver Tequila

1/2 oz Cynar

1/2 oz Ultimate Grapefruit Cordial (see page 192)

1/4 oz lime juice

2 1/2 oz premium soda

Fresh grapefruit slice, for garnish

*For this recipe, I recommend the Love of Cocktails salt rimmer, but feel free to substitute with another if you have an...

1 Distribute the cocktail rimmer onto a small plate and shake the plate to spread it evenly across the surface.

2 Cut the lime wedge and rub it around the rim and a bit of the sides of a 10-oz Collins glass. Take the glass and dip the rim and sides in the salt on the plate.

3 Add tequila, Cynar, cordial, and lime juice to the pre-rimmed glass.

4 Fill glass with ice and stir to dilute. Add more ice if needed and top with soda.

5 Garnish with the fresh grapefruit slice.

Pink Songbird

Inspired by a crisp Canadian cottage morning complete with singing songbirds, this cocktail is as bright and refreshing as a Muskoka sunrise. A combination of Canadian herbs with grapefruit and tonic, this cocktail is a perfect Spanish style G&T that you'll end up making every time.

1 oz Dillon's Unfiltered Gin 22

¼ oz Bigallet Thyme Liqueur

½ oz Ultimate Grapefruit Cordial (see page 192)

4 drops Pine and Spruce Tincture (see page 198)

3 oz premium dry tonic

Grapefruit twist, for garnish (see page 48)

Pine needles, for garnish (optional)

1 In a 13-oz wine glass, combine gin, liqueur, cordial, and tincture.

2 Add ice to fill the glass ¾ of the way.

3 Stir with a bar spoon to dilute, for about 10 seconds.

4 Add more ice to fill the wine glass and top with tonic.

5 Garnish with the grapefruit twist and pine needles.

Sunset in Venice

This adventurous, spritzy, fun, and low-ABV cocktail is a "choose your own adventure" style drink as it is best made when mandarin oranges are in season. Lambrusco, a sparkling Italian red, can also be a wild card, as it will range from deep hues of red (due to some producers' use of long grape skin contact during production) to a light whisper of pink for those producers who pull the liquid off the grapes sooner. I tend to choose a variety of Lambrusco from Chiarli Castelvetro for its black plum, blood orange, and allspice flavors. It is also tannic, rich in body, and relatively low in ABV.

½ sweet mandarin orange, sections taken out and seeded

2 sprigs tarragon (1 for garnish)

1½ oz Martini Bianco Vermouth

½ oz Easy Citrus Peel Cordial (see page 192)

¼ oz lemon juice

3 oz Lambrusco

1   In a cocktail shaker, muddle mandarin orange pieces and 1 sprig of tarragon.

2   Add vermouth, cordial, and lemon juice.

3   Add enough ice to cover the liquid in the shaker, plus a bit more.

4   Cover and shake vigorously for 10–15 seconds.

5   Strain through a Hawthorne strainer into a 12-oz rocks glass over freshly cracked ice.

6   Slowly pour in the Lambrusco and float it on top of the cocktail.

7   Garnish with the remaining tarragon sprig.

Watermelon Afternoon

When I was young, my nanny used to put out trays of fruit for me and my sister to snack on. My favorite was watermelon dipped in spiced Filipino salt, and the memory of that salty-sweet and spicy sensation has stayed with me to this day. Similarly, I hope this salty-sweet and icy cocktail—with notes of watermelon, raspberries, bitter orange, and a touch of salinity—lingers memorably on your lips for years to come.

1 oz Absolut Watermelon Vodka

1 oz Aperol

¾ oz Herbed Raspberry Shrub (see page 194)*

3 drops Saline Solution (see page 203)

¼ cup watermelon cubes

Large watermelon slice, for garnish

*For this recipe, I recommend mint as your herb of choice for your shrub.

1   In a Ninja Foodi power blender (or similar), combine vodka, Aperol, shrub, and saline solution.

2   Add watermelon cubes and ½ cup ice.

3   Turn blender on to medium and blend until smooth.

4   Pour into a 12-oz Collins glass.

5   Garnish with the watermelon slice.

Bittersweet Symphony

Inspired by our family's visits to Niagara wine country—where I was first introduced to the sweet, sweet nectar of Icewine grapes—this cocktail is bittersweet and harmonious, with flavors of honey and dark fruits, as well as a refreshing hit of effervescence from the sparkling wine topper. Underutilized in the cocktail world, Icewine provides drinks with beautiful texture and natural sweetness.

1 oz VQA Cabernet Franc Icewine

½ oz Campari

½ oz passion fruit juice

½ oz lime juice

2 oz Freixenet Carta Nevada Brut Cava Sparkling Wine

1 In a cocktail shaker, combine all ingredients but the sparkling wine.

2 Add enough ice to cover the liquid in the shaker, plus a bit more.

3 Cover and shake vigorously for 10–15 seconds.

4 Strain through a Hawthorne strainer into a 12-oz wine glass.

5 Slowly top with sparkling wine and give the drink a quick stir with a bar spoon.

Icewine is made from late-harvest grapes left on the vine in cold climate wine-producing areas. Grapes are carefully harvested when frozen, then pressed. The freezing of the grapes concentrates the sugars, resulting in a luscious, intensely flavored product with an unbelievable balance of sweetness and acidity.

The Great Grape Parade

This drink is one that my event-planning partner and dear friend Christina and I keep on the back burner in case of a cocktail emergency, and it never disappoints. Essentially a Pisco Mojito Royale (to "royale" a drink simply means adding sparkling wine), this version of the beloved Mojito is unique in its grapes on grapes on grapes composition—distilled, fermented, and juiced. Grape lovers, line up!

½ lime, cut into quarters

6 seedless green grapes (3 to muddle, 3 for garnish)

1½ oz Peruvian pisco

½ oz Easy Rich Syrup (see page 184)

5-6 mint leaves

3 oz Freixenet Cordon Negro Brut Cava Sparkling Wine

1   In a cocktail shaker, muddle lime pieces and 3 green grapes until juices are released and fibers are broken down.

2   Add pisco and syrup.

3   Add enough ice to cover the liquid in the shaker, plus a bit more.

4   Cover and shake vigorously for 10–15 seconds.

5   Strain through a Hawthorne strainer into a 12-oz Collins glass.

6   In your palm, take mint leaves and clap to release oils. Add to the cocktail.

7   Fill glass with ice and stir with a bar spoon. Top with sparkling wine and stir again.

8   Garnish with a skewer of the remaining grapes.

THE WARM & FUZZIES

When cooking and eating, we all have our comfort food favorites—those dishes filled with warmth and familiarity. They are made with staple ingredients and feature simple yet robust flavors. The warm and fuzzies of the drinks world are similarly positioned. They are slow, simple sippers, shaken or stirred, sturdy and spirit forward, and often filled with a delightful combination of wood, earth, winter spices, and more. Think of a classic Old Fashioned, a smoky highball, or a perfectly chilled Martini. Now we're talkin'!

IN THIS CHAPTER...

Ready, Set, Play

This cocktail is a take on a Coffee and Tonic, made popular in Europe in the early 2000s, but with some added floral and bitter notes. Although it only contains four ingredients, the flavors—from floral to savory to bitter—are truly integrated and the balance of something bitter and bright is the exact reason why this cocktail can be both a digestif and an aperitif.

1½ oz Lavender Infused Bianco Vermouth (see page 201)

½ oz Cynar

1½ oz cold brew coffee (see Tip)

3 oz premium dry tonic

Lavender sprig, for garnish

1 In a 10-oz Collins glass, combine all ingredients but the tonic and lavender sprig.

2 Fill glass with ice and stir with a bar spoon for 10–15 seconds, until well chilled.

3 Add more ice and top with tonic.

4 Garnish with the lavender sprig.

TIP

For the cold brew coffee in this recipe, any store-bought kind will work, but if you wish to make your own, I would recommend doing a 4:1 water to coffee beans ratio. Take 1 cup of coffee beans and grind on the coarse setting. Combine ground coffee and 4 cups filtered water in a large container with a lid. Let sit in the refrigerator for 12 hours. Use a cheesecloth or coffee filter on a colander to strain out the grounds the next day. (Pour through again if necessary.) Serve cold and keep the remainder refrigerated.

Buio Americano

This easy three-ingredient cocktail is a chocolaty, coffee-enhanced version of a classic Americano. The addition of burnt orange ties the whole cocktail together, and it is so easy it can be ready in the matter of seconds. For low ABV fans, think of this as your ultimate aperitif that you can batch ahead of time and serve to your guests as an adult, liquid version of a chocolate orange.

1 oz Cacao Nib and Coffee Bean Infused Campari (see page 200)

½ oz Amaro Averna

4 oz sparkling water

Burnt orange zest, for garnish (see Tip)

1　In a 10-oz Collins glass, combine Campari infusion and amaro.

2　Fill glass with ice and stir with a bar spoon for 5–10 seconds.

3　Add more ice and top with sparkling water.

4　Garnish with the burnt orange zest.

TIP

To create a burnt orange zest, create an orange twist (see page 48). Light a torch, a lighter, or a match and hold it 2 to 3 inches above the cocktail. Using your other hand, hold your orange twist in between your thumb and forefinger and place it above the fire source with the outside of the peel facing the flame. Squeeze to release oils. The oil will hit the flame and ignite, creating a bright flame and, in the end, a burnt orange aroma for the drink. Place burnt orange zest in the drink to add an additional layer of charred goodness (or discard).

Sesame Vermouth and Tonic

This simple cocktail is inspired by a classic Vermouth and Tonic. One of my favorite tricks is to emphasize a flavor by layering the same tasting notes throughout a cocktail by having them appear in multiple expressions. In this drink I'm giving you nutty-on-nutty goodness, playing the marzipan and almond notes of the Amontillado Sherry off a bittersweet black sesame infused vermouth. The combination makes this aperitivo perfect for an early fall evening get-together.

¾ oz Toasted Sesame Infused Sweet Vermouth (see page 202)

¾ oz Amontillado Sherry

4 oz premium dry tonic

Lemon twist, for garnish (see page 48)

1 In a 10-oz Collins glass, combine vermouth infusion and Sherry.

2 Fill glass with ice and stir with a bar spoon for 5–10 seconds.

3 Add more ice and top with tonic.

4 Garnish with the lemon twist.

Cranberry Mamie

This smoky whisky highball with luscious cranberry notes is a reinvented version of the Mamie Taylor cocktail—an old-timey cocktail named after American actress Mayme Taylor, whose brush with stardom came at the end of the 1800s. With a hint of Fernet-Branca, this version brings out amazing notes of saffron and allspice with a touch of berry sweetness.

¾ oz Laphroaig Quarter Cask Scotch

¼ oz Fernet-Branca

½ oz tart cranberry juice*

4 oz premium dry ginger ale

Fresh cranberries, for garnish

Be sure that what you are using is cranberry juice and not cranberry cocktail!

1 In a 10-oz Collins glass, combine Scotch, Fernet-Branca, and cranberry juice.

2 Fill glass with ice and stir with a bar spoon for 5–10 seconds.

3 Add more ice and top with ginger ale.

4 Garnish with the fresh cranberries.

Truffled Alaska

In the restaurant industry, truffle season is always something to look forward to. The expensive, seasonal, and difficult-to-harvest fungi is a luxury ingredient. If you do get to experience all the fineness that comes with this earthy and musky edible spore, this Truffled Alaska cocktail has some seriously extensive flavors, perfect for wet Martini lovers.

1½ oz Spirit of York Aquavit

¾ oz Black Truffle Infused Dry Vermouth (see page 201)

1 bar spoon (½ Tbsp) Yellow Chartreuse

2 drops Saline Solution (see page 203)

Lemon peel, for aromatics (see Tip on page 111)

Black truffle flake, for garnish (see Tip)

1   In a mixing glass, combine all ingredients but the lemon peel and truffle flake.

2   Fill glass with ice and stir with a bar spoon for 10–15 seconds.

3   Strain through a Hawthorne strainer into a 5½-oz coupe glass.

4   Express the lemon peel overtop of the cocktail to add aromatics. Discard the peel and garnish with a black truffle flake.

Aquavit is a grain or potato spirit distilled or flavored with a variety of herbs. Often carrying notes of caraway, anise, or fennel, Aquavit is an adventurous graduation from a classic gin. If you can't source an Aquavit, you can substitute an herbal London Dry Gin (or an Old Tom for an added touch of sweetness) in its place. Try for a gin that leans toward the same herbal flavors.

TIP

Truffles may be hard to come by, but the point of this ingredient is to add some aromatics to the drink. To create a truffle flake, simply take a truffle bulb and slice it thinly on a mandoline or with a very sharp knife. It should sit floating on top of the drink. If truffles are not available, try adding a drop of truffle infused olive oil instead.

Green and Bitters

In my early bartending days, one of the first gin cocktails I was told to research was the Hanky Panky—invented by Ada Coleman, who in the early 1900s was the head bartender at the prestigious Savoy Hotel in London. It was a pivotal moment for female bartenders the world over. This version I'm offering you is lower in ABV than Ada's, and has flavors of orange, celery, and roots, and just the right amount of bitterness.

3 thin slices cucumber (about 1/6 inch)

1½ oz Manzanilla Sherry

½ oz Rutte Celery Gin*

½ oz Bigallet China-China Liqueur

1 bar spoon (½ Tbsp) Fernet-Branca

Celery curl, for garnish (see Tip)

*If not available, substitute with London Dry Gin and 2 dashes celery bitters.

1   In a mixing glass, slightly break apart cucumber slices with the edge of a bar spoon or tap lightly with a muddler.

2   Add the rest of the ingredients except the celery curl and fill glass with ice.

3   Stir with a bar spoon for 10–15 seconds.

4   Strain through a Hawthorne strainer as well as a fine cone strainer so no cucumber bits are left in the drink. Pour into a 5½-oz coupe glass.

5   Garnish with the celery curl.

TIP

To make a celery curl, use the same process as making a rhubarb curl. Place a single stalk of celery, ribbed side up, on a cutting board. Take a potato peeler and peel lengthwise, discarding the top pieces. Repeat until you have a long smooth strip you can twist into itself and secure with a cocktail pick.

Open Sesame

When we talk about comfort food in Asia, we talk about hot pot. The communal and conversational nature of sharing food cooked in one pot of spicy herbal broth is one of my favorite things. And the best part is adding your own individual flavors by making sauces on the side; mine are always sesame heavy. This cocktail is a cool digestif with a savory bitterness that is perfect for hot pot—or any gatherings, for that matter!

1½ oz Monkey Shoulder Scotch

¾ oz Toasted Sesame Infused Sweet Vermouth (see page 202)

¼ oz Benedictine

3 dashes Bittered Sling Moondog Latin Bitters

Black sesame oil, for garnish

Lemon peel, for aromatics (see Tip)

1   Put a 5½-oz coupe glass in the freezer to chill.

2   In a mixing glass, combine all ingredients but the sesame oil and lemon peel.

3   Fill glass with ice and stir with a bar spoon for 10–15 seconds.

4   Strain through a Hawthorne strainer into your chilled coupe glass.

5   Garnish with 3–4 drops of black sesame oil. Express the lemon peel overtop to add aromatics. Discard the peel.

TIP

To express a citrus peel, hold it between your thumb and forefinger, point the outer peel in the direction of the drink, and squeeze slightly so the oils release. Immediately you will be able to smell the aroma of the citrus oils, which adds a zesty fragrance to any cocktail.

Open Sesame, p. 111

Queen Barbarella

A modified version of the popular cocktail I once had on an experimental cocktail bar's menu. Named after Jane Fonda's sexually progressive, open, and empowering character Barbarella, in the movie of the same name, this cocktail is spirit forward, strong, and vibrant, with unique fruit notes.

1½ oz Del Maguey Tobala Mezcal

¾ oz bianco vermouth

¼ oz Herbed Raspberry Shrub (see page 194)

4 dashes Bittered Sling Malagasy Chocolate Bitters

Curled rhubarb stalk, for garnish (see Tip on page 59)

1 Put a 5½-oz coupe glass in the freezer to chill.

2 In a mixing glass, combine all ingredients but the rhubarb stalk.

3 Fill mixing glass with ice and stir with a bar spoon for 10–15 seconds.

4 Strain through a Hawthorne strainer into your chilled coupe glass.

5 Garnish with the curled rhubarb stalk.

Winter in Niagara

The pride and joy of the Niagara region of Canada is Icewine. And while it may take more effort to produce, the resulting silky-sweet nectar is totally worth it. Icewine adds body, acidity, and a great depth of flavor to shaken or stirred cocktails while also contributing tree fruit notes, like peach and apricot, as well as distinct smokiness and evergreen qualities. If you've not been to the Niagara region in the winter, this drink will definitely transport you there.

Sprig of rosemary

1 oz Lot No. 40
100% Pot Still Rye Whisky

½ oz VQA Vidal Icewine

½ oz dry vermouth

¼ oz Odd Society
Mia Amata Amaro*

¼ oz Green Chartreuse

Amaro Nonino will provide a similar nutty flavor, only lighter.

1   Use a lighter to carefully char the rosemary sprig. Place the still-smoking sprig in the center of a non-reactive plate.

2   Cover the sprig with an upside-down mixing glass, letting the smoke fill the glass until it subsides (about a minute).

3   Flip the mixing glass right side up and immediately add the rest of the ingredients.

4   Add enough ice to cover the liquid, plus a bit more. Use a bar spoon to stir for 10–15 seconds.

5   Strain through a Hawthorne strainer into a 5½-oz coupe glass.

6   Garnish with your charred rosemary sprig.

Pineapple Blanco

My version of this bittersweet cocktail brightens it up without sacrificing its spirit-forward nature. "Blanco" simply means white, and while this stirred cocktail is dry, it also packs a nice tropical punch with notes of pineapple and bittersweet lemon, along with herbal, rooty flavors of gentian, and some salinity from the Sherry.

1 oz Pineapple Infused Sombra Mezcal (see page 202)

½ oz Fino Sherry

¾ oz Affino Aperitivo*

½ oz Martini Bianco Vermouth

Lemon peel, for aromatics (see Tip on page 111)

Dehydrated pineapple chip, for garnish

You could also use a gentian liqueur like Suze.

1   In a 12-oz rocks glass, combine all ingredients but the lemon peel and dehydrated pineapple chip.

2   Fill the glass with ice. Use a bar spoon to stir for 10–15 seconds. Add more ice to fill (if necessary).

3   Express the lemon peel overtop of the cocktail to add aromatics. Discard the peel and garnish with a dehydrated pineapple chip.

Smoked Maple Old Fashioned

I think any cocktail enthusiast has had an Old Fashioned or two during their time. My spin on this celebrated classic carries notes of warm maple and smoke, which adds depth to the aromatics from the Angostura Bitters and bourbon. The fun aspect of this cocktail is that your choice of bourbon will ultimately shape the characteristics of the finished drink. I've opted for a bourbon with a corn-heavy mash for added sweetness. But feel free to explore! This recipe is so good I made it into a cocktail kit for my company, Love of Cocktails.

6–7 applewood chips

2 oz Woodford Reserve Bourbon

¼ oz dark maple syrup

2 dashes Angostura Bitters

2 dashes Bittered Sling Plum & Rootbeer Bitters

Dehydrated orange wheel, for garnish (see page 48)

1   Pile your applewood chips in the center of a non-reactive plate. Use a lighter to carefully set the cluster of applewood chips on fire. Let the pile form a small flame.

2   Cover the smoldering chips with an upside-down 12-oz rocks glass, letting the smoke fill the glass until the fire subsides (about a minute).

3   In a mixing glass, combine all remaining ingredients but the dehydrated orange wheel.

4   Fill the mixing glass with ice. Use a bar spoon to stir for 10–15 seconds.

5   Turn your smoke-filled glass over and add a large cube of ice. Strain the contents of the mixing glass through a Hawthorne strainer into the smoked glass and over the ice.

6   Garnish with the dehydrated orange wheel.

Apple Alpine Old Fashioned

A fruit-forward, bitter bourbon cocktail that has just the right amount of sweetness from the whiskey mash and apple brandy. This stirred cocktail has loads of depth to it, with a touch of saltiness and pleasant alpine notes that make it a fantastic spin on an Old Fashioned.

1 oz Rittenhouse Straight Rye

¾ oz Boulard Calvados Pays d'Auge Brandy

¼ oz Braulio Amaro Alpino (see Tip)

¼ oz cloudy apple juice

Pine twig with needles, for garnish

1   Put a 12-oz rocks glass in the freezer to chill.

2   In a mixing glass, combine all ingredients but the pine twig.

3   Fill with ice and use a bar spoon to stir for 10–15 seconds.

4   Strain through a Hawthorne strainer into the chilled rocks glass over a large ice cube.

5   Garnish with the pine twig.

TIP

Braulio Amaro Alpino is an Italian herbal liqueur made with a blend of roots, herbs, and berries, with a predominantly citrus-spruce aroma of lemon verbena, spruce tips, and basil. If it is not available, another bitter-forward amaro would work, like Fernet-Branca Menta.

Guerrilla Girls

The Guerrilla Girls are an anonymous group of activist feminist artists who fight sexism and racism in the art world. In my world of beverage alcohol, whiskey is perhaps the realm most dominated by men, and this cocktail, inspired by the never-ending fight of the Guerrilla Girls, is aimed at empowering the women of whiskey. Simply put, this is a stiff drink with bold intentions and flavors that are universal and intriguing.

1½ oz Lot No. 40
100% Pot Still Rye Whisky

¾ oz Amaro Lucano

½ oz dry vermouth

8 drops Bittered Sling
Lem-Marrakech Bitters

Lemon square, for garnish
(see page 48)

1 In a mixing glass, combine all ingredients but the lemon square.

2 Fill the glass with ice. Use a bar spoon to stir for 10–15 seconds.

3 Strain through a Hawthorne strainer into a 12-oz rocks glass over fresh ice.

4 Garnish with the lemon square.

The Eddy

While I thought it strange at the time, one of my father's favorite combinations was honeyed Japanese green tea and blended Scotch. Looking back on it now, I must admit, my dad was on to something. The floral expression that comes from some blended Scotches mingles tantalizingly with the slight earthiness found in Japanese tea. This is a beautiful warming drink. Make sure you raise a glass to Eddy when you're sipping this one.

1 bar spoon (½ Tbsp) matcha powder

2 oz Chivas Regal 12 Year Old Scotch

¼ oz St-Germain Elderflower Liqueur

1 bar spoon (½ Tbsp) Easy Rich Syrup (see page 184)

2 dashes Bittered Sling Kensington Aromatic Bitters

Lemon flower, for garnish (see page 48)

1   In a 12-oz rocks glass, use a matcha whisk (see Tip) to combine matcha powder and ¼ oz water until a slight paste forms and all clumps are broken down.

2   Add all remaining ingredients but the lemon flower.

3   Fill glass with ice and stir with a bar spoon for 10–15 seconds.

4   Garnish with the lemon flower.

TIP

A matcha whisk (or chasen) is a bamboo whisk made specially for combining fine matcha powder with liquid. Matcha powder is, simply, very finely ground Japanese green tea leaves that are dried under cover to preserve the vibrancy and freshness. Unlike other powders, though, it is ultra-fine and usually takes aeration and a whisk to integrate. Hence the use of the matcha whisk, which is superior to other whisks because of its numerous and concentrated tines. In a pinch, a small, standard whisk will work in this recipe, especially because you are making a paste and not a tea.

Black Cat Alley

When we lived in Hong Kong, there was a cobblestone staircase in an alley my sister and I used on our route home from school. On these walks we'd dawdle and poke our heads into the local street food stalls. While I can't remember the name of the alley, the smells of deliciously toasted, smoky, and sugared chestnuts and ginger custards have stayed with me. So too does the memory of the chestnut stall owner's black cat. It would sit there peacefully as customers came and went with their bags of toasty goodness. Black Cat Alley is a perfect little sipper that commemorates those moments.

1 oz Lagavulin
8 Year Old Scotch

½ oz Spanish sweet vermouth

¼ oz Edmond Briottet
Crème de Châtaigne
Chestnut Liqueur

¼ oz Ginger Rich Syrup
(see page 184)

¾ oz lemon juice

1 roasted and shelled chestnut,
for garnish (see Tip)

1 In a cocktail shaker, combine all ingredients but the chestnut.

2 Add enough ice to cover the liquid in the shaker, plus a bit more.

3 Cover and shake vigorously for 10–15 seconds.

4 Strain through a Hawthorne strainer into a 12-oz rocks glass over fresh ice.

5 Garnish with the roasted chestnut.

TIP

Roasted and shelled chestnuts are available to be purchased at many local grocers, but if you wish to make your own, the steps are easy. Preheat an oven to 425°F. Using a sharp knife, make an X incision in the flat side of each chestnut shell. Fill a pot with cold water and the prepared chestnuts. Bring to a boil. Remove chestnuts after boiling for 5 minutes. Arrange chestnuts in a single layer on a baking sheet and roast in preheated oven for 15–20 minutes. Remove and let cool fully before shelling.

Afternoon Martini

This lusciously creamy, sweet and spiced version of an espresso Martini is definitely a dessert-like drink, but sometimes you just gotta treat yourself. Amirite? So, when you do decide to treat yourself, luxuriate in the rich flavors of this crowd pleaser.

¾ oz Vodkow Classic Cream Liquor

1 oz Chai Tea Infused Vodkow Vodka (see page 203)

1 oz brewed espresso

¼ oz Vanilla Agave Syrup (see page 189)

Ground chai tea leaves, for garnish

1 In a cocktail shaker, combine all ingredients but the tea leaves.

2 Add enough ice to cover the liquid in the shaker, plus a bit more.

3 Cover and shake vigorously for 10–15 seconds.

4 Strain through a Hawthorne strainer into a 7-oz coupe glass.

5 Garnish by sprinkling tea leaves on top.

Hops 'n' Robbers

This simple sour celebrates the outstanding craft beer culture in Toronto. Some florality, cocoa, and deep bitterness make this a fantastic sipper for any day. I particularly love the pairing of hops with the earthiness of a reposado tequila, which contributes some vanilla and woody quality to this sour.

1 oz Tequila Tromba Añejo

¾ oz Braulio Amaro Alpino

½ oz IPA Reduction
(see page 187)

1 oz lemon juice

4 drops Ms. Better's Bitters
Miraculous Foamer

3 drops Bittered Sling
Grapefruit & Hops Bitters

Grapefruit flower, for garnish
(see page 48)

1   In a cocktail shaker, combine all ingredients but the grapefruit twist.

2   Cover and dry shake without ice to aerate the liquid and create a bit of frothiness.

3   Add enough ice to cover the liquid in the shaker, plus a bit more.

4   Cover and shake vigorously for 10–15 seconds.

5   Strain through a Hawthorne strainer into a 12-oz rocks glass over a large ice cube.

6   Garnish with the grapefruit flower.

The Miraculous Foamer used in this recipe is a vegan alternative to using egg whites. If you choose to substitute egg whites for the foamer, the 4 drops is equivalent to one egg white. Follow the directions above and the drink will froth just the same.

The Deep Flip

A flip is a cocktail that contains a full egg. In the 1600s people made flips with beer, rum, and sugar. Now, I am not normally a flip person, but sometimes deep in the winter when the days are short and the cold is bracing, a flip is exactly what I need! I like to consider it a dessert-type drink—a sophisticated take on an eggnog. My version has notes of coffee, raisin, and toffee and a touch of earthiness.

1 oz Diplomatico Reserva Exclusiva Rum

½ oz Pedro Ximénez Sherry

½ oz Amaro Averna

¼ oz Coffee Demerara Syrup (see page 189)

1 whole egg

Nutmeg, for garnish

Cocoa powder, for garnish

1 In a cocktail shaker, combine all ingredients but the nutmeg and cocoa.

2 Cover and dry shake without ice to break down the egg.

3 Add enough ice to cover the liquid in the shaker, plus a bit more.

4 Cover and shake vigorously for 10–15 seconds.

5 Strain through a Hawthorne strainer into a 5-oz coupe glass.

6 Garnish with a slight dusting of nutmeg and cocoa powder.

Spiced Hot Cider

Nothing gives me the warm and fuzzies more than a nice hot cider, especially when I'm curled up with a blanket by the fire. This version combines the warming flavors of brandy with apples. It's extremely easy to make batches of this drink. So, throw it into a thermos and bring it along for your cold-weather outdoor adventures.

4 cardamom pods

4 oz apple cider

1 stick cinnamon

1 oz pear eau-de-vie

½ oz Cocchi Americano

½ oz lemon juice

1 bar spoon (½ Tbsp) orange marmalade

Burnt orange zest, for garnish (see Tip on page 105)

1   In a heat-proof mug, lightly muddle cardamom pods.

2   Add apple cider and cinnamon stick. Cover and heat in the microwave for 2 minutes on high.

3   Carefully take off the lid. Add eau-de-vie, Cocchi Americano, lemon juice, and orange marmalade.

4   Stir to integrate flavors.

5   Garnish with the burnt orange zest.

Banana Yuen Yeung

Growing up I was particularly fond of a Chinese beverage we used to have for breakfast called yuen yeung—it is a mixture of Hong Kong–style milk tea (incredibly strong black tea mixed with milk) and coffee. It is seven parts milk tea to three parts coffee. The balance of tannins, roasted coffee, and creamy milk is something I still daydream about. This cocktail is pretty much an adult, boozy version of yuen yeung with added flavors of banana and honey. You're welcome!

3 oz heavily steeped black tea

1 oz Maker's Mark Bourbon

¼ oz Giffard Banane du Brésil Liqueur

¼ oz Lignum Coffee Blossom Honey

2 dashes Bittered Sling Arabica Coffee Bitters

Brûléed banana slice, for garnish (see Tip)

1   Make a cup of strong black tea, from which you will get your 3 oz.

2   In a heat-proof mug, combine bourbon, banana liqueur, honey, and bitters. Stir and mix well.

3   Slowly pour in the black tea and stir until integrated.

4   Garnish with the brûléed banana slice.

> **TIP**
>
> To brûlée a banana slice, take one slice of fresh banana and sprinkle white sugar on top. Take a torch or a lighter and apply the flame to the banana slice until caramelized.

White Lily Toddy

When it comes to hot drinks, dark spirits tend to take center stage. However, I like to mix things up, and, alcoholic or not, one of my favorite warm beverages is a nice white tea. So, why not add some spirited delights? This hot gin punch is perfect for those rainy spring days where you can smell the flowers from a mile away.

1 Tbsp baihao yinzhen white tea

1 oz Fonseca White Port

½ oz Plymouth Gin

¼ oz Best Base Honey Syrup
(see page 186)

¼ oz lemon juice

Long lemon twist, for garnish
(see page 48)

1 Steep 1 cup of the white tea following the instructions of the tea producer.

2 In a large heat-proof mug, combine Port, gin, syrup, and lemon juice. Stir and mix well.

3 Add white tea and stir until integrated.

4 Garnish with the lemon twist.

Baihao yinzhen tea is a style of Chinese white tea also known as White Hair Silver Needle and is produced in the Fujian province of China. It is of extremely high quality and carries the floral aroma of lilies.

TEMPERANCE INQUISITIVE & CANNA-CURIOUS

This chapter is all about drink inclusivity. Choosing a cocktail without alcohol (or even without alternative additives like cannabis) should still feel like sipping on a carefully considered drink. Gone are the days of the Shirley Temples, welcome to sophisticated non-alcoholic options with serious flavors and surprising expressions that will challenge your palate!

IN THIS CHAPTER...

Cannabis cocktails have been such a fantastic category to explore. Cannabis is loaded with terpenes—natural compounds responsible for the way things smell—as are many things in the spirits and wine world (like pine, lavender, and orange, to name a few). So, it only makes sense to explore the expressions cannabis can bring to cocktails. The cannabis-inclusive cocktails in this book are made for those who are canna-curious. Please do measure carefully as dosages affect every individual differently. THC and CBD are both cannabinoids found in the cannabis plant. THC can bind to CB1 receptors in the brain and can provide the intoxicating "high" sensation. While CBD does not impair function, they are both psychoactive. Start with a low dosage, as suggested in the recipes, and increase with tolerance and proper measures. As with all cocktails, enjoy responsibly.

Smoked 'No'mericano

Inspired by the classic Americano cocktail—a sparkling bitter Italian aperitivo and vermouth combination—this highball style 'No'mericano has smoky black tea paired with a bitter aperitivo, offering a balance of bitterness from rhubarb root, bitter orange, gentian, and chinchona bark.

2 oz lapsang souchong tea
(see Tip)

½ oz Easy Citrus Peel Cordial
(see page 192)

1 oz Novara Non-Alcoholic
Aperitivo

4 oz sparkling water

Lemon twist, for garnish
(see page 48)

Orange twist, for garnish
(see page 48)

1 In a 10-oz Collins glass, combine lapsang souchong tea, cordial, and aperitivo and fill with ice.

2 Stir lightly and add sparkling water.

3 Stir to integrate bubbles and top with more ice, if needed.

4 Garnish with the lemon and orange twists.

TIP

Brew the tea according to the tea producer's instructions. However, in my experience the ratio should be 1 teaspoon for every 3½ ounces of water. Steep for 3 or 4 minutes.

Red Mystique

This easy, Royale-style cocktail is the perfect temperance digestif. Chinotto, popular as a carbonated beverage in Italy, is produced from the juice of the fruit from a myrtle-leaf orange tree. There are many renditions of Chinotto, some light in color and some more floral, and yet others that are bittersweet like cola.

2 oz Chinotto Reduction (see page 189)

4 oz Grüvi Non-Alcoholic Prosecco

Olive, for garnish

Grapefruit twist, for garnish (see page 48)

1   To a 12-oz Collins glass, add the Chinotto reduction and fill with ice.

2   Stir lightly with a bar spoon and slowly add the non-alcoholic Prosecco.

3   Stir to integrate bubbles and top with more ice, if needed.

4   Garnish with the olive and grapefruit twist.

Cashew Colada

This non-alcoholic cocktail combines two of my favorite guilty pleasure cocktails: a Mai Tai and a Pina Colada! So, let's whip up a creamy, dreamy, tropical treat that the whole gang will love.

1 oz Lyre's White Cane Spirit

3/4 oz Cashew Orgeat (see page 186)

1/4 cup cubed pineapple

1 1/2 oz coconut milk

1/2 oz lime juice

Pineapple fronds, for garnish

1 In a Ninja Foodi power blender (or similar), combine all ingredients but the pineapple fronds.

2 Add 1/4 cup ice and blend on medium (or the "smoothie" function) until smooth.

3 Pour contents into a 10-oz rocks glass. (Or a tiki glass if you have one!)

4 Top with cracked ice if needed and garnish with pineapple fronds.

Feathered Dreams

This cocktail is herbal and citrus forward, combining Seedlip Grove's orange, ginger, and lemongrass notes with a touch of salinity. Try pouring this into a popsicle mold and freezing for a non-alcoholic, super fresh summer snack.

1 oz Seedlip Grove 42

¾ oz Chamomile and Meyer Lemon Syrup (see page 187)

½ oz lemon juice

3 oz aloe vera juice

Lemon twist, for garnish

1   In a cocktail shaker, combine all ingredients but the lemon twist.

2   Add enough ice to cover the liquid in the shaker, plus a bit more.

3   Cover and shake vigorously for 10–15 seconds.

4   Strain through a Hawthorne strainer into a 10-oz Collins glass filled with ice.

5   Garnish with the lemon twist.

Aloe vera juice derives from the aloe plant, and comes from the leafy part. It contains antioxidants and is great for inflammatory issues, and is a digestive aid. It has a slightly bittersweet taste and provides great citrus qualities.

Zero Hero

This stirred hero cocktail (a cocktail that can be the main character on any drink menu) will save the day with flavors of allspice, clove, and salted grapefruit. Verjus is a tart, grape-based ingredient that you can use to elongate any drink, and is particularly useful in adding depth to non-alcoholic concoctions.

1 oz Seedlip Spice 94

3/4 oz Featherstone 12 Brix Verjus

1/2 oz Ultimate Grapefruit Cordial (see page 192)

2 drops Saline Solution (see page 203)

Grapefruit peel, trimmed, for garnish

1 In a mixing glass, combine all ingredients but the grapefruit twist.

2 Add enough ice to cover the liquid in the mixing glass, plus a bit more.

3 Stir with a bar spoon for 10–15 seconds until well chilled.

4 Strain through a Hawthorne strainer into a 5 1/2-oz coupe glass

5 Garnish with the grapefruit peel.

The word "verjus" comes from the French term *vert jus*, literally meaning "green juice." Vintners select and pick grapes in early harvest that won't make the cut for winemaking because of their high acid and low sugar content and the pressing of these early harvest grapes becomes verjus. Any verjus that is bone dry would work, but I use a variety from a local winery with herbal and tannic Cabernet Franc grapes that measure at 12 Brix sugar content, which is a fancy way of saying the resulting juice is very dry and tart.

The Deep Dive

A Sangria-style cocktail that is tart with some great acidity from cranberry juice, while also being berry forward. The non-alcoholic wine I've chosen is from Acid League and I picked it because of its notes of cherry, blueberry, coffee, and oak. However, you can use any non-alcoholic dry red wine. This one is deep in flavor.

2 oz Acid League Proxies Velvet Non-Alcoholic Red

½ oz Herbed Raspberry Shrub (see page 194)

½ oz tart cranberry juice*

1 tsp blackberry jam

Herb-blackberry skewer, for garnish (see page 49)

Be sure that what you are using is cranberry juice and not cranberry cocktail!

1 In a cocktail shaker, combine all ingredients but the herb-blackberry skewer.

2 Cover and shake to break down the jam.

3 Add enough ice to cover the liquid in the shaker, plus a bit more.

4 Cover and shake vigorously for 10–15 seconds.

5 Pour contents into a 13-oz wine glass and add cracked ice to top off the glass.

6 Garnish with the herb-blackberry skewer (using the herb of your choice).

Spring on First Ave.

My first trip to New York was in the spring of 2016. I couldn't believe the beauty and the hustle of the city, and the uniqueness of each area. The boutique hotel I stayed in was in the Lower East Side off First Avenue. That trip was taken when kombucha was all the rage. I remember visiting a café with an abundant selection and was blown away. This non-alcoholic highball has just the right amount of fruity freshness, with some bright acidity, and subtle ginger spice. I've used a kombucha from a local female-owned producer here in Toronto, but feel free to experiment with different styles—and different shrubs!

¾ oz Lumette! London Dry

¾ oz Rhubarb Saffron Shrub (see page 195)

4 oz Moore Lemongrass Ginger Kombucha

Rhubarb stalk, for garnish

1   In a 10-oz Collins glass, combine London Dry and shrub.

2   Fill with ice and stir with a bar spoon for 10–15 seconds.

3   Top with the kombucha.

4   Garnish with the stalk of rhubarb.

Not a Pumpkin Spice Latte

Who needs a #PSL when this winter-ready, Hot Toddy–style cocktail can fill your pumpkin craving? Bursting with pleasant textures, flavors, and bitterness, this easy-peasy drink whips up in minutes. Simply put everything in the microwave or heat up a big batch on the stove for the perfect warming nip with friends 'round the fire.

Juice of ¼ lemon

½ oz Lyre's American Malt

½ oz Chinotto Reduction (see page 189)

4 oz apple cider

1 tsp pumpkin purée

Grated nutmeg, for garnish

1 In a cocktail shaker, combine all ingredients but the nutmeg.

2 Cover and dry shake until pumpkin purée is broken down, about 5–10 seconds.

3 Pour contents into a heat-proof mug.

4 Cover with plastic wrap and microwave on high for 2 minutes. (Or heat on medium in a pot on the stove.)

5 Garnish with grated nutmeg.

Green Bird of Paradise

This flavor-bomb of a cocktail combines tropical honeyed notes with matcha and some maltiness from a cannabis beer-like beverage with 1.5 milligrams each of CBD and THC per can. In the 3 ounces used in this cocktail, there would be about 0.65 milligrams of each.

½ tsp matcha powder*

½ oz filtered water

Pulp from 1 purple passion fruit (see Tip)

½ oz Best Base Honey Syrup (see page 186)

¼ oz yuzu juice

3 oz Truss Beverage Co. Mollo™ 5

*See page 124 for a tip on how to whisk matcha powder.

1   In a cocktail shaker, use a matcha whisk to combine the matcha powder and filtered water. Whisk until you've created a tea with a thicker consistency.

2   Add passion fruit pulp, syrup, and yuzu juice.

3   Add enough ice to cover the liquid in the shaker, plus a bit more.

4   Cover and shake vigorously for 10–15 seconds.

5   Strain through a Hawthorne strainer into a 14-oz wine glass and top with more ice.

6   Top with Mollo™ 5 and give it a quick stir with a bar spoon to integrate.

TIP

When picking passion fruit, look for ones that feel a bit heavy—the skin can be smooth or wrinkly. Give the whole fruit a good wash to remove any wax or pesticide residue, then cut in half. Take a spoon and simply scoop out the pulp (seeds included) to use.

The New Cosmo Fizz, p. 156 and Green Bird of Paradise, p. 154

The New Cosmo Fizz

There was a time in the drinks world that if it was pink, it was a Cosmo (or Cosmopolitan, to be more accurate). *Sex and the City* was all the rage, then. I remember being infatuated with the outrageous outfits and Cosmos. To be a writer like Carrie Bradshaw—doing it all and living her life in the city—was so appealing to me. Now that I understand what it is like being a writer (it's hard!), I can see why so many Cosmos were needed. My life may not be full of impossible-to-put-on dresses and Christian Louboutin pumps, but it is relatively complete with this low-THC cannabis beverage (5 milligrams THC), which has become something of a writing aid. Featuring a combination of cranberry, citrus, and bitter orange, this New Cosmo Fizz is perfect in length, texture, and taste. Write on!

½ oz Tuscan Tree
Non-Alcoholic Aperitivo Spirit

1 oz blood orange juice

½ oz Ultimate Grapefruit
Cordial (see page 192)

4 oz House of Terpenes™
Canntinis Cranberry Citrus
Cosmo

Fresh orange slice, for garnish

1   In a 12-oz Collins glass, combine Tuscan Tree Non-Alcoholic Aperitivo, blood orange juice, and cordial.

2   Fill glass with ice and stir with a bar spoon for 5–10 seconds.

3   Slowly top the drink with House of Terpenes™ Canntinis Cranberry Citrus Cosmo.

4   Give it a quick stir to integrate the fizz into the drink.

5   Garnish with the fresh orange slice.

Tuscan Tree Non-Alcoholic Aperitivo is a zero-percent ABV distilled spirit infused with blood orange and botanicals. In this cocktail it adds some depth and structure with its riff on a classic Italian aperitif.

Pink Panther

This fresh and floral number contains 0.65 milligrams of CBD and 0.65 milligrams of THC and features notes of lemon, tangerine, and thyme paired with acid adjusted grapefruit. This salted Paloma-style cocktail with tons of citrus components is mouthwateringly good.

½ oz Hibiscus and Pink Peppercorn Rich Syrup (see page 185)

¾ oz Acid Adjusted Grapefruit Juice (see page 195)

2 drops Saline Solution (see page 203)

3 oz Little Victory™ Sparkling Blood Orange Beverage

Grapefruit wedge, for garnish

1   In a 10-oz rocks glass, combine syrup, acid adjusted grapefruit juice, and saline solution.

2   Fill glass with ice and stir with a bar spoon for 10–15 seconds to dilute.

3   Top with Little Victory™ Sparkling Blood Orange Beverage. Stir to integrate and top with cracked ice.

4   Garnish with the grapefruit wedge.

Makrut Smash

Done in the style of a classic smash recipe—a julep with leafy herbs (usually mint) and fruit—this fun and distinctive twist provides beautiful evergreen and citrus flavors. Topping them with House of Terpenes™ Canntinis Ginger Lime Mule creates a funky-fresh drink that is aromatic and full of zing. Contains 5 milligrams of THC per drink.

2 makrut lime leaves (1 julienned, 1 whole for garnish)

3 slices cucumber (coins ⅛ inch thick)

½ lime, cut into quarters

¼ oz Vanilla Agave Syrup (see page 189)

4 oz House of Terpenes™ Canntinis Ginger Lime Mule (divided)

1   In a 10-oz rocks glass, combine julienned lime leaf, cucumber slices, lime pieces, and syrup.

2   Muddle to break down cucumber and release lime juices and fragrance from lime leaf.

3   Add ice to fill half the glass and add 2 oz of the House of Terpenes™ Canntinis Ginger Lime Mule. Stir with a bar spoon to integrate. Top with more ice.

4   Top with the remaining 2 oz House of Terpenes™ Canntinis Ginger Lime Mule and give it a quick stir with a bar spoon to integrate.

5   Garnish with the remaining lime leaf.

The Island Lounger

When I think of relaxing on an island, my mind conjures up a warm ocean breeze, luscious fruit, the smell of suntan lotion, and, of course, the welcome drink often served at tropical resorts. The Island Lounger is a canna-curious, sophisticated take on that welcome drink. Filled with mouthwateringly sweet citrus and stone fruits, and containing 3.4 milligrams THC and 1.7 milligrams CBD, this drink will welcome you to cannabis beverage delights.

½ lime, cut into quarters

½ oz Best Base Honey Syrup (see page 186)

3–4 mint leaves

1 oz mango nectar

4 oz Sweet Justice Pacific Island Punch (divided)

1 mint sprig, for garnish

1   In a mixing glass, combine lime pieces and syrup. Muddle to release lime juices.

2   Take mint leaves and place them in the middle of your palm. Clap to release oils and add leaves to mixing glass.

3   Add the mango nectar and 2 oz of the Sweet Justice Pacific Island Punch.

4   Add enough ice to cover the liquid in the mixing glass, plus a bit more.

5   Use a bar spoon to stir lightly for 5–10 seconds.

6   Strain through a Hawthorne strainer as well as a fine cone strainer into a 12-oz Collins glass filled with ice.

7   Top with the remaining 2 oz Sweet Justice Pacific Island Punch and give it a quick stir to integrate.

8   Garnish with the mint sprig.

My Ruby Cola

This savory, tart, and earthy cannabis cocktail explodes with flavors of turmeric, cherry, and ginger. The Sweet Justice OG Cola has the classic taste of sarsaparilla, some earthiness and allspice notes, and imparts only 1 milligram of THC in this drink (of the 3.5 milligrams in the full can). Think of this as your canna-cherry cola riff for those who are just starting to experiment with cannabis cocktails. It's delicious!

1½ oz pure cherry juice

½ oz Ginger Rich Syrup (see page 184)

½ oz lemon juice

Pinch of turmeric powder

3 oz Sweet Justice OG Cola

1 In a cocktail shaker, combine all ingredients but the Sweet Justice OG Cola.

2 Add enough ice to cover the liquid in the shaker, plus a bit more.

3 Cover and shake vigorously for 10–15 seconds.

4 Strain through a Hawthorne strainer into a 12-oz Collins glass.

5 Slowly top with the Sweet Justice OG Cola and give it a stir with a bar spoon to integrate.

Field of Dreams

If you have ever been through a field of flowering elderberry trees, you will know that the scent is truly, unbelievably dreamy. In the alcohol world, we have St-Germain Elderflower Liqueur as our famed floral additive to drinks. In the cannabis world, there is Elderflower Pom from Sweet Justice, which has just the right amount of fragrance and a zesty tang that comes from the pomegranate juice. It is a perfectly dreamy canna-curious sip. Here I have upped the ante by adding chamomile to enhance those flavors—making one heck of an aperitif cannabis cocktail, with only 1.7 milligrams THC and 1.7 milligrams CBD.

½ oz Chamomile and Meyer Lemon Syrup (see page 187)

½ oz lemon juice

4 oz Sweet Justice Elderflower Pom (divided)

Lemon square, for garnish (see page 48)

1 In a 10-oz Collins glass, combine syrup, lemon juice, and 2 oz of the Sweet Justice Elderflower Pom.

2 Fill with ice and stir with a bar spoon for 5–10 seconds.

3 Slowly top the drink with the remaining 2 oz Sweet Justice Elderflower Pom.

4 Give it a quick stir to integrate the fizz into the drink.

5 Garnish with the lemon square.

TELL YOUR FRIENDS TO ROLL UP

This chapter is filled with large-format servings, from tea punches to non-alcoholic pitchers—these recipes are ready to party! If you make them ahead of time, the ingredients and flavors will become more integrated as time passes, just like a good stew. Most recipes have some tips for substitutions if you're in a pinch and a full grocery run isn't in the books. More importantly, have fun, make a mess, and tell your friends to roll on up!

Group G&T

Everyone should have an easy party trick up their sleeves for impromptu get-togethers. So, I'm sharing mine with you—a self-serve pitcher of G&T! This quick infused version is a crowd pleaser, and if you keep my cordial handy in the fridge, your friends will be blown away with the perfect blend of botanicals and cucumber freshness. Put out some short Collins glasses and tonic and your hosting will go from good to great!

10 oz London Dry Gin

5 oz Manzanilla Sherry

4 sprigs tarragon

¼ cup sliced fennel

3 grapefruit peels (about 2 inches long, plus more for garnishes)

4 oz Cucumber Lime Cordial (see page 193)

Chilled premium dry tonic or elderflower tonic (about 30 oz total, or to guests' taste)

Citrus wheels, for garnishes (optional)

Fresh herbs, for garnishes (optional)

SERVES ABOUT 10 COCKTAILS

1   In a large jug (at least 64 oz in volume), combine gin, Sherry, tarragon, and fennel. Slightly muddle the tarragon and fennel to release oils and juices. Toss in grapefruit peels (expressed first, see Tip) and let sit to infuse for an hour—though the longer it sits the more flavor it takes on.

2   Before serving, add cordial and fill the pitcher with ice and stir.

3   Pour into small Collins glasses packed with ice. Leave room for guests to top with about 3 oz of tonic.

4   Place additional pre-cut grapefruit peels, citrus wheels, and fresh herbs in a bowl beside the pitcher so guests can self-garnish.

Baby Pear Punch

This one is fresh and fun, filled with pear, honey, and allspice notes—
and it's non-alcoholic! I recommend using a large punch bowl so
some infused aromatics can be added in if you wish. Add a few large
ice cubes to the punch, rather than small ones, for slower dilution.
This punch can also be served warm. Simply ladle the punch into
a mason jar with plastic wrap to cover and heat it up on low in the
microwave for a couple of minutes.

4-5 sprigs thyme

10 oz Seedlip Spice 94

1 lemon, cut into thin slices

½ Bartlett pear, cut into
thin slices

10 oz pear juice

5 oz apple cider

5 oz Best Base Honey Syrup
(see page 186)

5 oz lemon juice

20 oz chilled green tea
(see Tip)

SERVES ABOUT 10 COCKTAILS

1   Use a lighter to lightly toast the thyme sprigs until fragrant.
    Blow out any flames and place the toasted sprigs in a large
    punch bowl (at least 128 oz in volume).

2   Add Seedlip Spice 94.

3   Add lemon and pear slices. Stir and let sit for 10-15 minutes
    to infuse.

4   Add the rest of the ingredients and give it a stir. (The chilled
    green tea will dilute the punch in place of water.)

5   Add a few giant ice cubes and stir. Serve immediately by
    ladling into small punch cups.

TIP

For best results, steep your green tea in
hot water according to the tea producer's
instructions. Once complete, remove tea
leaves and let tea cool before chilling.

Spiced Berry Beret

An explosion of berry flavors paired with reposado tequila, this Sangria-inspired punch is too good to last the entire party! My mother used to make Sangria with cinnamon infused orange juice, cassis, and boxed wine. While I always thought it was an amazing party trick, I never admitted that to her. So, this is an ode to my mother, and the many pitchers of Sangria I snuck a taste from. Have fun and make lots of substitutions—anything goes with this one.

3 cups mixed berries, such as blackberries and raspberries

10 oz Patron Reposado Tequila

20 oz dry red wine

2 cinnamon sticks

½ orange, sliced into wheels

5 oz Vanilla Agave Syrup (see page 189)

10 oz Acid Adjusted Pineapple Juice (see page 195)

20 oz premium soda

SERVES ABOUT 10 COCKTAILS

1   In a large punch bowl (at least 128 oz in volume), combine mixed berries, tequila, and wine. Take a wooden spoon and gently mash the berries and let sit for at least 1 hour.

2   Add cinnamon sticks, orange slices, syrup, and acid adjusted pineapple juice and give it a stir.

3   Add a large ice chunk or a couple of large ice cubes and pour in the soda. Serve immediately by ladling the cocktail into rocks glasses filled with ice.

> TIP
>
> This is an easy one to play with. No berries? Use peaches. No red? Use white. Be creative and don't be shy in exploring flavor pairings!

Green Haka Cooler

I absolutely love kiwis, and this delicious summer-ready cocktail is super simple to throw into a punch bowl and go. It's made with fresh, acidic Muscadet wine, bianco vermouth, and verjus—and the prep is relatively minimal. Exchange the bianco vermouth for dry vermouth for a grassier finish, or swap it out for a cachaça for a higher ABV punch.

3 kiwis, sliced

2 limes, sliced into wheels

10 oz bianco vermouth

5 oz St-Germain Elderflower Liqueur

20 oz Muscadet Sur Lie

5 oz Easy Citrus Peel Cordial (see page 192)

8 oz Featherstone 12 Brix Verjus

SERVES ABOUT 10 COCKTAILS

1   In a large punch bowl (at least 128 oz in volume), combine all ingredients.

2   Stir to integrate flavors and chill in the refrigerator until ready to serve.

3   Before serving, give it a quick stir. Add a few giant ice cubes to maintain temperature.

4   Serve immediately by ladling into small punch cups.

> **TIP**
>
> If you would like to lengthen this punch to serve more people, you can add the juice of 1 whole lime and 10 oz pear cider. Other things to consider adding to the base recipe are Topo Chico Twist of Lime Mineral Water or tepache (see page 204) for some extra sweetness. You can also consider lime wedge garnishes.

Watermelon Whip

This watermelon punch is ridiculously fresh. It is almost like it has an unfair advantage because the flavors in this recipe are like matches made in heaven. Feel free to substitute a light blanco rum or a light juniper gin, or even Absolut Citron Vodka for some added zestiness, in place of the pisco.

10 oz Fino Sherry

5 oz Chilean pisco

½ oz absinthe

5 oz watermelon juice

5 oz Ultimate Grapefruit Cordial (see page 192)

10 drops Saline Solution (see page 203)

1 cup watermelon cubes

10 mint sprigs (15–20 leaves for punch, mint sprig tips for garnish)

10 oz Freixenet Cordon Negro Brut Cava

SERVES ABOUT 10 COCKTAILS

1   In a large punch bowl (at least 128 oz in volume), combine all ingredients but the Cava and mint sprig tips.

2   Stir to integrate and chill in the refrigerator until ready to serve.

3   Before serving, pour in Cava and give it a quick stir. Add a few giant ice cubes to maintain temperature.

4   Serve immediately by ladling into small punch cups. Garnish cups with mint sprig tips.

Easiest Milk Punch Ever

Milk punches are time consuming, I know. But they are also one of the easiest ways to pre-batch some delicious flavors with luscious texture. The best part about a milk punch is that it is great pre-bottled. So, try this uniquely smoky-sweet number to wow your friends when you show up at the next party! My recommendation is to have it rest a full 24 hours before you plan to consume it. Not a fan of mezcal? Substitute a blanco tequila or a blanco rum and it's still an absolute stunner.

8 oz mezcal

8 oz Coconut Infused
Amontillado Sherry
(see page 199)

Peels of 2 lemons

4 cardamom pods

2 star anise pods

4 oz lemon juice

4 oz pineapple juice

2 oz Giffard Apricot Brandy

4 oz Easy Citrus Peel Cordial
(see page 192)

8 oz steeped black tea

8 oz whole fat milk, cold

Grated nutmeg, for garnish

SERVES ABOUT 10 COCKTAILS

1   Combine all ingredients but the milk and nutmeg in a container and let sit for 3–4 hours to infuse. Once infused, strain out solids.

2   To a separate non-reactive container, add the milk.

3   Slowly pour the cocktail mixture into the milk. Stir gently. The milk will begin to curdle.

4   It is integral that you are patient with this process. Let sit for up to 12 hours in the refrigerator. Do not stir. Milk solids will completely separate, leaving the flavored whey. You can leave it for up to 24 hours.

5   Line a large container with a fine cone strainer and a piece of cheesecloth. Strain mixture through and discard remaining separated milk solids

6   Sanitize another large container with a large mouth opening. Place a coffee filter in a fine cone strainer over the mouth. Pour the strained liquid through the coffee filter and cone strainer into your serving vessel to get the smaller milk particles out. If any cloudiness remains, strain one more time.

7   Bottle milk punch and refrigerate. It will keep up to 3 weeks.

8   Serve in small rocks glasses filled with ice and garnish with grated nutmeg if desired.

Shanghai Tea Party

I used to love gok fa cha—chrysanthemum tea sweetened with rock sugar—as a kid. This delightful and floral punch is made with memories of gok fa cha. Tie guan yin (a style of Chinese tea with notes of creamy, fruity, and vegetal qualities) along with gin, vermouth, Scotch, and lemon—not to mention chrysanthemum—this punch makes my inner child happy!

10 oz London Dry Gin

5 oz bianco vermouth

3 oz Monkey Shoulder Scotch

10 oz Chamomile and Meyer Lemon Syrup (see page 187)

5 oz lemon juice

20 oz chilled tie guan yin (see Tip)

¼ cup chrysanthemum flowers, for garnish

¼ cup lemon verbena leaves, for garnish

SERVES ABOUT 10 COCKTAILS

1 In a large pitcher (at least 60 oz in volume), combine all ingredients but the flowers and verbena leaves and stir to combine.

2 Let chill in the refrigerator until ready to serve.

3 Before serving, give it a quick stir. Add a few giant ice cubes to maintain temperature.

4 Serve immediately by pouring into small rocks glasses filled with ice. Garnish with the flowers and verbena leaves.

TIP

For best results, steep your tea in hot water according to the tea producer's instructions. Once complete, remove tea leaves and let it cool before chilling.

The Last Tropical Fix

I mean, we can't not have a rum punch, can we? The problem with standard rum punches is that they are very sweet and often full of artificial ingredients. So, here is a genuine rum punch without any artificial crap. By using one of my drinking vinegar recipes and an aperitivo, this Jungle Bird–like mix pairs the bitter notes of Campari with fruit juices to give you your tropical fix.

5 oz Worthy Park Single Estate Reserve Jamaican Rum

5 oz Sailor Jerry Spiced Rum

5 oz Campari

8 oz Herbed Raspberry Shrub (see page 194)

4 oz lime juice

10 oz passion fruit juice

2 oz Angostura Bitters

2 cups raspberries, for garnish

2 sliced limes, for garnish

SERVES ABOUT 10 COCKTAILS

1 In a large pitcher (at least 60 oz in volume), combine all ingredients but the raspberries and lime slices and stir to combine.

2 Let chill in the refrigerator until ready to serve.

3 Before serving, give it a quick stir. Pack the jug full of ice cubes for dilution and to maintain temperature.

4 Serve immediately by pouring into small rocks glasses filled with ice. Garnish with the raspberries and lime slices.

SH*T
I PUT IN
EVERYTHING

Creating a next-level cocktail requires a depth of flavor and dimension that is impossible to get by simply mixing base spirits and something fizzy. Sweet, sour, bitter, salty, umami, hot, and cold are all flavors and sensations that help to create something magical in your glass when blended expertly with select base spirits and quality lengtheners. So with that, I present to you some of my most celebrated syrups, tinctures, and shrubs—the sh*t I put in *everything*—that have helped me create some award-winning cocktails, and that are essential for outstanding alcoholic and non-alcoholic drinks alike. Many of these ingredients appear multiple times in this book, and some will take longer than others to execute. But trust me, the prep is all worth it!

SWEETENERS

Sugar is a cocktail staple. Sweetness can come in many varieties, and in this chapter, I'll cover the expected (my take on simple syrup) and the unexpected (a nut-based milk syrup, for one example). There are so many possible flavor combinations out there. Use what I provide in the following pages as a guide and have fun creating your own special blends.

Easy Rich Syrup

COOK TIME: 15 MINUTES | YIELD: 2 CUPS

This recipe will stand as your base sugar syrup that can be altered with various flavors, a few of which I highlight below. (You can also add this to your morning coffee instead of granulated sugar.) This "rich" simple syrup is called so because it is twice as sweet as a classic simple syrup. I prefer using rich syrup because it yields a stronger flavor profile without additional liquid.

2 cups white granulated sugar

1 cup water

1. In a small saucepan, combine sugar and water and heat on medium-low.

2. Stir until sugar is completely dissolved, scraping the sides with your spatula to avoid crystallization.

3. Let the syrup cool and pour into a non-reactive container. Store at room temperature for two weeks or in the refrigerator for four months.

Enhanced Rich Syrups

Easy Rich Syrup is a great base to use to create some of your own flavors. Don't fuss too much about the measurements, it's all about experimentation. Mostly, you can simply infuse this syrup with any edible ingredient (stick with fruits, vegetables, herbs, and teas to start) by adding a bit to step 1 of the recipe. You can also take some of the yield of your Easy Rich Syrup and make smaller portions of flavored syrup. Below are some of my favorite additions and some varying techniques for infusion.

GINGER RICH SYRUP Ginger root provides a spicy-sweet brightness to cocktails. Add 1 Tbsp of fresh-pressed ginger juice to 2/3 cup of Easy Rich Syrup in a blender. Blend to integrate ginger juice with the rich syrup. Bottle and refrigerate for up to 1 month, before the ginger taste starts changing. Shake well before use each time. YIELDS 2/3 CUP

CHAI RICH SYRUP Chai imparts an aromatic, allspice-like flavor to cocktails. For Chai Rich Syrup, add in 5 tsp of chai black tea leaves and two 2-inch strips of orange peel in step 1. Continue with the recipe instructions. When done, strain through a fine strainer. Let cool; bottle and refrigerate for up to 2 months. YIELDS 2 CUPS

UBE RICH SYRUP Ube is a purple yam popular in Filipino cooking. Its extract has an earthy, candied, vanilla-like flavor, which can be beautiful in cocktails. For Ube Rich Syrup, add 3 drops of ube extract to ½ cup of Easy Rich Syrup. Whisk with a fork to blend ube extract with syrup. Bottle and refrigerate for up to 3 months. Shake well before use each time. YIELDS ½ CUP

CARAMELIZED BANANA PEEL RICH SYRUP
Caramelized banana peel will add a toasted sweetness to your cocktails. For Caramelized Banana Peel Rich Syrup, you need the peel of 1 banana (you can eat the banana). Cut the peel into small slices, add to a saucepan, and sauté over medium-high heat for a couple of minutes. Add 1 cinnamon stick and 1 cup of sugar to the saucepan and stir until sugar coats the peels. Add ½ cup of water and reduce the heat to medium. Stir until sugars are diluted. Strain out solids. Let cool; bottle and refrigerate for up to 3 weeks. YIELDS ⅔ CUP

MUGICHA RICH SYRUP Mugicha is Japanese barley tea, which is made from roasted un-hulled barley kernels. It is like what is used in beer brewing. Mugicha imparts a toasted, bitter flavor to cocktails. For Mugicha Rich Syrup, toast 1 Tbsp of mugicha in a small saucepan on medium heat until fragrant, about 2–3 minutes. Add 1 cup of water, then add 2 cups of granulated white sugar. Continue with the recipe instructions. When done, strain out solids using a fine strainer. Let cool; bottle and refrigerate for up to 2 months. YIELDS 2 CUPS

HIBISCUS AND PINK PEPPERCORN RICH SYRUP
Hibiscus flowers provide a sweet and tart flavor to cocktails, and also add a vibrant red hue to anything you cook them with. Pink peppercorns provide a slight bite that has more aromatic, subtly sweet spice than black peppercorns. For Hibiscus and Pink Peppercorn Rich Syrup, add in 1 Tbsp of Hibiscus flower petals and 1 tsp of pink peppercorns in step 1 of the recipe. Continue with the recipe instructions. When done, strain through a fine strainer. Let cool; bottle and refrigerate for up to 2 months. YIELDS 2 CUPS

Cashew Orgeat

PREPARATION TIME: 5 MINUTES | YIELD: 2 CUPS

Orgeat is typically an almond and floral syrup for tiki-style drinks like a Mai Tai. This is an almond-free alternative using cashew milk. Use it to add texture and creaminess to your cocktails so you can skip the dairy. A splash is also great to sweeten your morning coffee.

1¼ cup unsweetened cashew milk

2 cups white granulated sugar

1 tsp rose water

1. In a Ninja Foodi power blender (or similar), combine cashew milk and sugar.

2. Cover and start your blender on medium-low for 2–3 minutes. Slowly rise to medium speed and blend for another 2–3 minutes.

3. Check that the sugar has dissolved in the cashew milk. Test this by dipping a spoon in the mixture. Let the mixture drip off the spoon and check the back for sugar granules. If the sugar is not fully dissolved, continue blending and checking until it is.

4. Once sugar is fully incorporated, add rose water. Pulse blender a few times to integrate it. Bottle and refrigerate for up to 3 weeks.

TIP

This recipe also works to create syrups using unsweetened rice milk, which will give your cocktails a delightful floral note, or oat milk, which will impart a more earthy, cereal flavor. For either one, use the same proportion as the cashew milk.

Best Base Honey Syrup

COOK TIME: 15 MINUTES | YIELD: 2 3/4 CUPS

There are many grades of honey and for something that I have named "the best," you best believe that the quality of the honey plays an important role! An added touch of funkiness from bee pollen helps take this syrup to the next level. Get ready to add this to everything from a Bee's Knees to a classic Hot Toddy—even your next salad dressing.

1 cup water

3/4 tsp bee pollen

2 cups Lignum Coffee Blossom Honey (or other high-grade amber honey)

1. In a small saucepan, bring water to a simmer over medium-high heat. Add bee pollen and stir.

2. Add the honey and turn heat to low.

3. Stir until honey is integrated and bee pollen is dissolved.

4. Fine strain out all solids using a cheesecloth on a colander and let cool. Bottle and refrigerate for up to 3 months.

Chamomile and Meyer Lemon Syrup

COOK TIME: 30 MINUTES | YIELD: 2 CUPS

This floral and subtly tart combo is fantastic for shaken or stirred cocktails. Chamomile provides subtle apple notes with a mellow honey-like sweetness, while Meyer lemon has a gentler citrus flavor than regular lemon and delivers some floral qualities, too. This combo is deadly!

3-4 Meyer lemons (see Tip)
2 cups white granulated sugar
3/4 cup strong brewed chamomile tea (see Tip)

1. Peel the lemons and place the peels in a medium bowl. Add sugar. Slightly muddle to release the oils from the peels. Set aside.

2. Cut the lemons in half and juice using an elbow juicer, saving 1/4 cup of the juice.

3. In a medium saucepan, combine the lemon peel and sugar mixture with the juice and the chamomile tea.

4. Bring to a simmer on medium heat then reduce to medium-low, stirring frequently until sugars are dissolved, about 10-15 minutes.

5. Let syrup cool and strain out solids. Bottle and refrigerate for up to 3 weeks.

> **TIP**
>
> To make chamomile tea, you can follow the instructions on the package, but I like to double the required tea. My go-to is 2 tea bags per 1 cup of hot water and brew for 4 minutes. If Meyer lemons are not readily available, use regular lemons but adjust your sugar quantity to account for the added tartness.

IPA Reduction

COOK TIME: 20 MINUTES | YIELD: 3/4 CUP

For the beer lovers out there, this reduction is a lovely way to get some hop and malts into cocktails for a surprising flavor burst. It also goes amazingly with anything agave.

3/4 cup hoppy IPA
1/2 cup agave nectar

1. In a small saucepan, bring IPA to a simmer on medium heat.

2. Let liquid reduce by half (about 15 minutes), then add agave nectar.

3. Whisk to integrate and let reduce for another 5 minutes on low.

4. Let reduction cool, then bottle and refrigerate for up to 3 months.

Chinotto Reduction

COOK TIME: 25 MINUTES | YIELD: 1 1/4 CUPS

This reduction of Italian soda is excellent for flavoring non-alcoholic and alcoholic cocktails alike. Sweet, with some floral, rooty notes, along with an added citrus blast from the citrus peels, this reduction is right at home in an aperitivo—simply add soda or try it in my Red Mystique cocktail on page 142. I have used the standard Chinotto soda Brio in this recipe, but you can use whatever type of bitter Italian soda you prefer. The additional herbs and peels in this recipe create a nice amaro alternative.

355 ml can of Brio Chinotto Italian Soda

2 bay leaves

4 grapefruit peels (each 2 inches long)

2 lemon peels (each 2 inches long)

3 cardamom pods, slightly cracked

3/4 cup white granulated sugar

1/2 tsp citric acid

1. In a small saucepan, heat Brio on medium until it starts to simmer, to reduce the carbonation and extract more flavor.

2. Add bay leaves, citrus peels, and cardamom pods.

3. Stir, reduce heat to medium-low, and let simmer for 20 minutes until the volume has reduced to about half. Add sugar and continue stirring until it has all dissolved.

4. Add citric acid and whisk in until combined.

5. Let cool completely, then strain out solids through a fine strainer, pressing to squeeze out excess. Bottle and refrigerate for up to 3 weeks.

SUPER QUICK, NO-COOK SYRUPS

Looking for big flavor in a hurry? Here are a couple of easy syrups with only a few ingredients that you can make in a matter of minutes!

Vanilla Agave Syrup: Take 1/2 cup of pure agave nectar and mix with 1/4 cup of hot water in a non-reactive container. Whisk until well integrated. Add 3 drops of bourbon vanilla extract. Whisk again. Bottle and refrigerate for up to 3 weeks. Yields 3/4 cup.

Coffee Demerara Syrup: Put 1/2 cup of hot coffee in a mason jar and add 1 cup of brown sugar. Seal the jar. Use a cloth or oven mitts to hold the jar. Shake vigorously until all sugar is dissolved. Let syrup cool, then bottle and refrigerate for up to 3 weeks. Yields 2/3 cup.

FRUIT CORDIALS & SHRUBS

There's nothing like a touch of tartness to really make a cocktail pop. These recipes will add acid and brightness to your cocktails while also allowing you to add subtle fruit flavors without adding the actual juice, or added volume, to your drink. Sometimes you just need that extra kiss of flavor and the ingredients below will do exactly that, all while rounding out the other unique components of your cocktails.

Easy Citrus Peel Cordial

PREPARATION TIME: 12-24 HOURS | YIELD: 2/3 CUP

If you're a citrus lover like me who tends to always add acidity to your regular cooking, you'll probably have some lemons, limes, and/or oranges in your fridge. But before you juice the flesh, take a second and peel off the skins, as the fragrant, delicious oils contained within create cocktail magic when mixed with sugar! This is my version of an all-fruits-are-welcome oleo-saccharum—a fancy term meaning "oil sugar" in Latin.

1 cup mixed citrus peels from washed citrus fruits (about 4 oz)

¾ cup white granulated sugar

⅓ cup hot water (about 175°F)

½ tsp malic acid

1. In a mason jar, combine citrus peels and sugar. Muddle the citrus peels to release oils and integrate with sugar.

2. Cover tightly and agitate by shaking the jar vigorously for 10–15 seconds. Let sit for 5 hours and agitate again. Oils from the peels should now have started dissolving the sugars slightly. The longer it sits, the better the flavors.

3. After 12 hours (or longer), open the mason jar, give it a quick stir, and add the water and malic acid. The latter will round out the citrus qualities.

4. Cover and shake again so all the elements are integrated and sugars are dissolved.

5. Strain out all the solids. Bottle and refrigerate for up to 3 weeks.

Ultimate Grapefruit Cordial

COOK TIME: 20 MINUTES | YIELD: 2 CUPS

I love a good grapefruit drink—there's something about the touch of bitterness in this citrus that is incomparable to the rest of the citrus family. It's varied insides—from white to ruby red to pink flesh—add nice tang and juiciness and the peels offer a delightful floral note. This cordial combines both flesh and peel elements and is great for a classic Paloma or to add some freshness to an Aperol Spritz.

Peel of 1 ruby red grapefruit, cut in 2-inch strips

1¾ cups white granulated sugar

3 whole cloves

4 allspice berries

1¼ cups ruby red grapefruit juice (from about 2 large grapefruits*)

1 tsp citric acid

*Use the extra peel for your Easy Citrus Peel Cordial.

1. Combine grapefruit peels with sugar in a medium bowl. Slightly muddle to release the oils and integrate with sugar. Set aside.

2. In a medium saucepan, toast cloves and allspice berries on medium heat until fragrant (about 3-4 minutes). Slowly add in grapefruit juice, then the sugar with peels and the citric acid.

3. Simmer on medium-low, stirring frequently until sugars are dissolved, about 10–15 minutes.

4. Let cool and strain out solids. Bottle and refrigerate for up to 3 months.

Cucumber Lime Cordial

PREPARATION TIME: 30 MINUTES | YIELD: 2 CUPS

This will be your new favorite thing! Cucumber—a vegetable that truly deserves a medal as the ultimate palate cleanser—is the star of the show. Its cool, refreshing, slightly herbal flavors are ideal for summer sippers. You can also enjoy this cordial paired with only some sparkling water or use it to enhance a delightful beverage that is low ABV.

3 large limes

1¾ cups white granulated sugar

1¼ cups cucumber juice (from about 1½ large English cucumbers) (see Tip)

1. Use a microplane and zest the skin of the limes and place in a medium bowl. Add in the sugar. Mix well and set aside for 15 minutes.

2. Cut the zested limes in half and juice with an elbow juicer to get ⅓ cup lime juice.

3. Transfer lime juice, cucumber juice, and sugar and lime zest mixture into a Ninja Foodi power blender (or similar). Blend on low-medium setting until sugar is dissolved (about 5 minutes).

4. Strain cordial through a fine sieve into a separate container, then seal and refrigerate for up to 3 weeks.

> **TIP**
>
> This recipe uses the cold extraction method: the syrup isn't cooked and the sugars dissolve due to the kinetic energy from blending. Cold extraction is perfect for preserving the freshness of the fruit and vegetables (cooked cucumbers are generally gross). Substitute cucumber with something like a green apple or celery and you'll yield the same delightful results.
>
> To juice cucumbers, cut cucumber into large chunks, and put through an extractor or cold press juicer for juice. To achieve maximum yield, the plump leftovers can be squeezed through a cheesecloth to extract the rest of the juice.

Herbed Raspberry Shrub

PREPARATION TIME: 24-48 HOURS | YIELD: 2 CUPS

A shrub is a drinking vinegar, and this easy-to-make version contains some serious flavors. Not only does it provide great acidity to your cocktail without needing citrus, it also makes a fantastic lengthener for a shandy (or other summer-ready drinks). The best part is this shrub can be made with your ugly or overripe raspberries so they don't go to waste!

1 cup ripe raspberries

1 cup apple cider vinegar

¾ cup Lignum Logwood Honey
(or other high quality all-natural raw honey)

¼ tsp chili powder

Handful of herbs, such as mint, basil, and/or tarragon

1. In a mason jar, muddle the raspberries to release flavors.

2. Add apple cider vinegar, honey, and chili powder. Stir until integrated.

3. Chop the herbs, add to the jar, and stir.

4. Seal mason jar and place in a cool, dark area. Allow flavors to infuse for 24–48 hours (the longer you wait, the more intense the flavors). Shake the jar 2–3 times during infusion.

5. Strain out solids. Bottle and refrigerate for up to 6 months.

Rhubarb Saffron Shrub

PREPARATION TIME: 3 1/2 HOURS | YIELD: 2 CUPS

Rhubarb season is my favorite! Not only does rhubarb pair well with pretty much anything from cinnamon to vanilla, it has a unique tartness that combines the best of both apple and cranberry and it takes amazingly well to sugar. Spruce up this fruity tartness by adding vinegar and some earthy, sweet, and floral saffron to it and you have yourself a shrub that you can easily use for drinking and cooking.

1½ cups chopped rhubarb

1 cup white granulated sugar

1 tsp Spanish saffron

¾ cup red wine vinegar

1. Add rhubarb, sugar, and saffron to a mason jar. Muddle to release flavors.

2. Let sit for 2–3 hours at room temperature so the sugar can take on some rhubarb flavor.

3. Transfer the contents of the mason jar to a saucepan and add the red wine vinegar.

4. Turn heat on low. Stir until sugars have dissolved and rhubarb fibers have broken down (about 15–20 minutes)

5. Remove from the heat and let cool.

6. Strain out all solids using a cheesecloth on a colander and squeeze out all excess liquid into your container.

7. Bottle and refrigerate for up to 6 months.

ACID ADJUSTED JUICES

You might have noticed that I've used citric and malic acid in some of the recipes. These acids enhance the tart and sour flavors of the fruit and citrus juices in the recipes. Both acids can be found in supermarkets and are readily available from online retailers. You can also use them outside of cordials by making acid adjusted juices that will pack a bit of an extra punch for a cocktail. By using the flavor of the juice, you are acidifying but not adding extra volume from say, a lime or a lemon. This protects the flavors of the other ingredients in your cocktail. Here are two I often use:

Acid Adjusted Pineapple Juice: Add 1 cup of canned pineapple juice and 2 tsp of citric acid to a high-powered blender. Pulse 2–3 times to dissolve citric acid. Bottle and refrigerate for up to 2 weeks. Yields 1 cup.

Acid Adjusted Grapefruit Juice: Add 1 cup of grapefruit juice, 1 tsp of citric acid, and ½ tsp of malic acid to a high-powered blender. Pulse 2–3 times to integrate acids. Bottle and refrigerate for up to 2 weeks. Yields 1 cup.

INFUSED & FUNKY THINGS

Infusing spirits with flavoring agents is a quick and easy way to limit the amount of ingredients you need for any one cocktail, and it will enable you to create impressively deep and robust flavors your friends will be asking after—and all it takes is just a few drops! As a general note, when straining solids you should always use a fine mesh strainer. And for those recipes that need extra fine straining, I've recommended you use a cheesecloth. After mastering these infusions you'll be well on your way to making your own recipes.

Pine and Spruce Tincture

PREPARATION TIME: 10-14 DAYS | YIELD: 1/2 CUP

This tincture is the ultimate scent of a fresh Canadian winter morning. It's like taking a walk through a pine forest. Just a few drops of this evergreen tincture will add mountains of flavor to the cocktails that call for it in this book, or even in your own classic Gin Martini. This one takes patience, but you'll be well rewarded for waiting.

1 Tbsp dried spruce tips (see Tip)
1 Tbsp dried pine needles (see Tip)
2/3 cup overproof vodka

1. Combine dried spruce tips and pine needles in a spice grinder or a food processor and slightly blitz.

2. To a non-reactive container, add vodka. Stir in ground spruce tips and pine needles and let sit at room temperature for at least 10 days, agitating a few times during the infusion period.

3. When the tincture reaches an intense flavor, strain out solids and bottle.

4. Store at room temperature. This tincture is shelf stable. To use it you can measure with a bar spoon or, if available, a medicine dropper.

TIP

Dried spruce tips and pine needles can be found in some specialized herb shops. However, if they aren't available you can easily make your own—but you'll need to pick them. For spruce tips you'll want to select the new sprig of growth at the end of the branch; they tend to be short and bright, often protected by a papery covering when they are young. Pine trees have many long needles and they are easily identifiable as each one comes out of a single point of origin. As far as taste goes, pine needles are warm, spicy, and sweet; spruce tips carry a citrus-forward flavor.

To dry spruce tips and pine needles, wash both stems and leaves thoroughly with warm water and pat dry with a paper towel. Place on a baking sheet lined with parchment paper and bake on low for 5-6 hours at 150°F to dehydrate fully. (Results may vary depending on oven.)

Coconut Infused Amontillado Sherry

PREPARATION TIME: 4-6 HOURS | YIELD: 2 1/3 CUPS

I make good use of Sherry in this book, the reason being that with lower alcohol alternatives on the rise, a cocktail with more than 2 ounces of spirits is harder to justify. While I do enjoy a high-ABV cocktail once in a while, it is important to find alternative ways to deliver depth of flavor and Amontillado Sherry is great for that (and it won't break the bank, either). Covering flavor profiles from stone fruit to melons, figs, nuts, and even some funk, this infusion is very versatile and adds a textural element to cocktails due to the coconut. I keep a bottle in my fridge at all times—and it's amazing on its own, chilled.

¼ cup large coconut flakes

2⅓ cups Amontillado Sherry

1. In a small saucepan, toast coconut flakes until oils are released and they look slightly beige. Transfer to a non-reactive container.

2. Immediately add in the Sherry.

3. Cover and put in the refrigerator for a minimum of 4 hours.

4. Strain out solids and pour through a coffee filter to remove any remaining oils.

5. Bottle and refrigerate for up to 3 weeks.

Nori Infused Fino Sherry

PREPARATION TIME: 12-24 HOURS | YIELD: 1 CUP

Here's a funky Sherry infusion for you. This one uses Fino Sherry, the pale and dry expression that is aged under a layer of flor (a natural biological film that during aging protects the Sherry from oxidation), and that has great brightness and acidity. Infusing it with the umami and sea salt flavors of seaweed makes for a remarkably light saline infusion with the slightest touch of nuttiness.

1 cup Fino Sherry

3 large pieces of unsalted dried seaweed (each about 3 inches x 4 inches)

1. In a large mason jar, combine the Sherry and the seaweed.

2. Cover and place in the refrigerator for 12-24 hours.

3. Fine strain out all solids using a cheesecloth on a colander and squeeze out all excess liquid into your container.

4. Bottle and refrigerate for up to 3 weeks.

Cacao Nib and Coffee Bean Infused Campari

COOK TIME: 1 HOUR | YIELD: 3/4 CUP

Who doesn't love a good Campari and soda? It's the ultimate two-ingredient highball for a bitter fan. Campari is a fantastic ingredient for a multitude of cocktails, and infusing this bittering additive with cacao nibs gives it a chocolaty taste without the sweetness and oils. Combining that with coffee beans adds a whole other layer of roasty complexity!

1 tsp coffee beans

1 tsp cacao nibs

1 cup Campari

1. Prepare a hot water bath by filling a medium-sized pot ¾ full with water. Bring water to a simmer.

2. Using a mortar and pestle, slightly crack the coffee beans.

3. In a small saucepan on medium heat, lightly toast cacao nibs to release flavor.

4. Transfer into a mason jar and add in the coffee beans. Immediately add in the Campari.

5. Seal jar and completely submerge in the hot water bath for 1 hour. Keep the bath at a low simmer.

6. Carefully remove mason jar and let cool.

7. Strain out solids and pour through a coffee filter to remove any remaining oils.

8. Bottle and refrigerate for up to 3 weeks.

Fig and Black Pepper Infused Cocchi Americano

COOK TIME: 25 MINUTES | YIELD: 1/2 CUP

This is an especially delightful infusion that I love enjoying on the rocks—or in the Fig Dreams cocktail on page 64! This infusion pairs one of my favorite fruits with an aperitivo filled with notes of baked apples, pears, honeysuckle, and orange blossom. The addition of black peppercorns highlights all those flavors, making this a "stick in your fridge and have it as dessert on the rocks" kind of infusion. Or, as one of my colleagues has tried, enjoy it with some beautiful, nutty cheeses.

1 large dried fig

2/3 cup Cocchi Americano

1/2 tsp black peppercorns

1. Prepare a hot water bath by filling a medium-sized pot ¾ full with water. Bring water to a simmer.

2. Chop the fig into quarters, then place them in a mason jar. Add the Cocchi Americano and peppercorns.

3. Seal jar and completely submerge in the hot water bath for 15–20 minutes. Keep the bath at a very low simmer.

4. Carefully remove mason jar and let cool.

5. Strain out solids. Bottle and refrigerate for up to 3 weeks.

Lavender Infused Bianco Vermouth

PREPARATION TIME: 3 HOURS | YIELD: 2/3 CUP

Bianco vermouth, also known as "vermouth blanc," sits somewhere between dry and sweet vermouths in terms of sweetness. Each brand has its own set of herbs and botanicals, but they all generally carry floral and wormwood flavors. This dried lavender infusion plays upon those floral qualities and adds an earthy tone. Want a lazy cocktail recipe? Simply have a couple ounces on the rocks with a splash of your favorite dry tonic. You won't regret it.

2/3 cup bianco vermouth
1 tsp dried lavender

1. In a mason jar, combine bianco vermouth and dried lavender.

2. Seal jar and let sit at room temperature to infuse for at least 3 hours.

3. Strain out solids. Bottle and refrigerate for up to 3 weeks.

Black Truffle Infused Dry Vermouth

COOK TIME: 2 1/2 HOURS | YIELD: 1 1/3 CUPS

Black truffle is such a delicacy. There's really nothing like it for the aromas and umami it will add to a dish or a drink. Pairing black truffle with dry vermouth not only brings earthiness to the fortified wine, but adds roundness and texture to your beverage. Try this in a Truffled Alaska on page 108.

3-4 slices black truffle (about 5 g)
1 1/2 cups dry vermouth

1. Prepare a hot water bath by filling a medium-sized pot 3/4 full with water. Bring water to a simmer.

2. Slice truffles, then transfer to a mason jar. Add the vermouth.

3. Seal jar and completely submerge in the hot water bath for 2 hours. Keep the bath at a low simmer.

4. Carefully remove the mason jar and let cool.

5. Strain out solids and pour through a coffee filter to remove any remaining oils.

6. Bottle and refrigerate for up to 3 weeks.

Toasted Sesame Infused Sweet Vermouth

PREPARATION TIME: 3 HOURS 10 MINUTES
YIELD: 2/3 CUP

Here's another interesting infusion using fortified wine. I've always found that sweet vermouth, no matter the brand, carries heartier notes of vanilla, caramel, and black fruits, with roots and barks on the end note. Sesame is such a huge part of Asian cuisine, providing a nutty and slightly bittersweet taste to savory and sweet dishes. Infusing the vermouth with sesame adds the most subtle depth to the mix.

1 tsp white sesame seeds
2/3 cup sweet vermouth

1. In a small saucepan, toast sesame seeds over low heat until fragrant and oils are released (about 5 minutes). Agitate often and be careful not to burn the seeds.

2. Remove from heat and immediately add the vermouth.

3. Transfer mixture to a mason jar. Seal jar and let sit to infuse for at least 3 hours.

4. Strain out solids. Bottle and refrigerate for up to 3 weeks.

Pineapple Infused Sombra Mezcal

PREPARATION TIME: 3 HOURS | YIELD: 2/3 CUP

Talk about a perfect pairing! This infusion adds tropical notes to an espadin mezcal that already has notes of vanilla, citrus peels, and green pepper. The addition of pineapple makes this a fantastic sipper on its own in a copita (a small clay cup used to sip mezcal) or in the Pineapple Blanco on page 118.

4 pineapple cubes (each about 1/2 inch square)
2/3 cup Sombra Mezcal

1. In a mason jar, muddle the pineapple cubes.

2. Add mezcal. Seal jar and let sit to infuse for at least 3 hours, agitating every so often (at least 3-5 times).

3. Strain out solids. Bottle and refrigerate for up to 6 months.

Chai Tea Infused Vodkow Vodka

PREPARATION TIME: 3 HOURS | YIELD: 2/3 CUP

When you think of fall and warming cocktails, we rarely reach for vodka. However, when this whey-based distillate is infused with chai tea (flavors of cinnamon, cardamom, ginger, cloves, and allspice), it is a perfect base for those heartier flavors. Use it to add a touch of depth to, say, a classic Moscow Mule, or in my Afternoon Martini on page 129.

1 tsp chai tea leaves (or 2 small tea bags)
2/3 cup Vodkow Vodka

1. In a mason jar, combine chai tea and vodka.

2. Seal jar and let sit to infuse for at least 3 hours, agitating every so often (at least 3–5 times).

3. Strain out solids and bottle. This infusion is shelf stable and can be stored at room temperature.

Saline Solution

PREPARATION TIME: 2 MINUTES | YIELD: 1/2 CUP

Like adding a pinch of salt to food, turning a pinch of high-quality salt into a measurable liquid is just enough to tie in and enhance the flavors of the other ingredients in a cocktail, creating depth and complexity.

100 g hot water (about 1/2 cup)
12.5 g Maldon salt (about 1 Tbsp + 1/4 tsp)

1. Boil water in a kettle to yield the 1/2 cup needed.

2. To a non-reactive container, add the hot water. Stir in the salt and mix until it has dissolved completely.

3. Let cool; bottle and store at room temperature. This saline solution is shelf stable.

Tepache

PREPARATION TIME: 48-72 HOURS | YIELD: 4 CUPS

This fermented pineapple beverage not only utilizes the parts of the pineapple you usually toss, but is great as a lengthener and carries tropical spiced notes. Best made in large batches and stored in the fridge, it can be used not just for cocktails, but on its own as a zesty, funky, non-alcoholic drink.

1 medium pineapple

8 cups warm water

1 cup soft brown sugar

¼ navel orange

1 large cinnamon stick

5 whole cloves

2 tsp ground nutmeg

1. Rinse the pineapple and brush off any dirt. With a large knife, carefully remove the crown of the pineapple, cut off the rind, remove the core, and set aside. Save the flesh for other uses.

2. In an extra-large mason jar or other non-reactive container, combine warm water and brown sugar and stir until sugar is dissolved.

3. Add pineapple rind and core along with the orange, cinnamon stick, cloves, and nutmeg.

4. Cover mason jar loosely with cheesecloth and screw on just the mason jar ring (no lid) to secure the cheesecloth.

5. Let sit for 48 hours at room temperature. Periodically check for foam forming on top of the mixture because of fermentation. Scoop the excess foam away.

6. After 48 hours taste the mixture. It should taste slightly fermented (which will have a funky and slightly carbonated taste/mouthfeel). If it does not have these qualities, seal the jar and check again in 24 hours.

7. When tepache is ready, strain out solids. Bottle and refrigerate to prevent further fermentation. Keep up to 1 week in the refrigerator.

ACKNOWLEDGEMENTS

I would like to extend the utmost gratitude to everyone who helped make this book happen.

To my editor, Steve, who held my hand with patience and guidance throughout this journey, thank you! Thank you as well to the fabulous designers at Figure 1, Naomi and Teresa, for executing my vision beautifully. I'd also like to express my gratitude to the rest of the Figure 1 team, who have simply been great to work with.

I'd like to raise a glass to Cocktail Emporium, who provided us with such beautiful glassware and tools to work with, and to all the hands that helped me style, organize, and produce the photos for this book. And of course, a huge shout out to my photographer, Jessica, who always knew what I wanted to convey in each picture.

To my beloved friends—especially Laura, Christina, and Dave—as well as to my Quell family of Trevor and Steph (and many more), thank you for always believing in me and pushing me to be my best. To my team at Ahma, Love of Cocktails, and SIMPL THINGS—especially Madison, Malik, and Erika—thank you for keeping the lights on and the wheels turning on my businesses while I took the time I needed to create this book.

To my parents Stella and Eddy, my sister Jacqueline, my grandparents, and the vibrant city of Hong Kong, thank you for your culture and encouragement. You have inspired my taste and stoked my creativity, for that I am forever grateful. To my partner, Justin, you have been such an important part of this journey and so many others. Thank you!

And to my previous, current, and future drink inspirators, thank you for giving me an outlet for my creativity and for allowing me to curate the unique experience that comes with each sip.

INDEX

ABOUT THE AUTHOR

EVELYN CHICK is a highly accredited specialist in the world of wine and spirits, and the anatomy of all things bar and beverage. She is globally recognized as a WSET Sommelier and Certified Specialist of Spirits and was also crowned Global Beefeater MIXLDN champion in 2015. Chick is a serial entrepreneur who combines her creative flair and sought-after business acumen to develop acclaimed bar experiences for media outlets, multimillion dollar venues, and notable brands. Chick is an advocate for the continued growth and sustainability of an inclusive and integrated food-and-drink community, leading the charge on creative zero-proof offerings and cannabis-infused cocktails.

Chick lives in the west end of Toronto, close to the Parkdale neighborhood where she is the founder of Ahma, a dynamic event and pop-up space, and her all-day cocktail and snack bar, SIMPL THINGS. Chick is also the founder of Love of Cocktails, where she and her team curate exciting beverage experiences from hosting cocktail classes, educational sessions, and tastings, to building premium cocktail gift sets for corporate and celebratory occasions. Quite simply, Chick is spreading the love of cocktails in each and every way possible.